Dear Anita,

We hope reading and cooking this book will be almost as mu— a real 2E2 cruise. Happy 50th

Thea & Alex

QE2

Queen Elizabeth 2 COOKBOOK

QE2

Queen Elizabeth 2 COOKBOOK

CAROL WRIGHT

Michael Joseph, London

First published in Great Britain in 1983 by
Michael Joseph Ltd., 44 Bedford Square, London WC1

Produced for Michael Joseph Ltd.,
by Gulliver Publishing Co. Ltd.

Design by Zena Flax Associates

ISBN 0 7181 2312 3

Printed and bound by
South China Printing Co., Hong Kong

Contents

List of Plates

INTRODUCTION
Three Million Meals a Year

The 67,107 ton liner, the *Queen Elizabeth 2,* is the world's largest à la carte restaurant providing daily meals at sea for up to 1,850 passengers plus 995 crew; a total of around three million meals a year.

Cunard has always been noted for what one American writer of the 'thirties called 'open handed hospitality' and in spite of a greater interest in health, most passengers indulge their food fantasies while on board, in anything from 1 lb steaks to 2½ inch veal chops. Some arrive with favourite recipes to challenge the chefs; others are persuaded to try something new and exotic as a change from steak and salad. Up to 40 per cent of dining is from special order lists; recipes like Chateaubriand, Beef Wellington, Rack of Lamb, Duckling à l'Orange, lobster or turbot with luscious sauces, or a complete Chinese, Japanese or Indian meal. In addition to the regular kitchen staff of 137, guest chefs from different countries join cruises to prepare specialities from their homelands.

With such a massive daily menu to prepare and no handy, mid-ocean supermarket to supply a strange spice or a fresh piece of fruit, storage on this floating city is extensive. The chef receives regular reports of the availability of fresh foods in ports around the world and telexes ahead for supplies; 200 tons of food from Los Angeles; 250 tons from Sydney, including fresh oysters on a World Cruise, and more food from Hong Kong and Singapore where fresh fruit and vegetables are flown in from Australia and the States. The Executive Chef, John Bainbridge, starts preparing his orders six months ahead of sailing on the World Cruise for which 500 tons of food are needed even before departure — 350 tons of food-stuffs and 150 tons of drink.

The amount of food taken on board even for a single transatlantic round trip is breathtaking: 2,000 lb biscuits, 800 dozen jars of marmalade, a mile of sausages, 500,000 tea bags, 50 lb dog biscuits, 22,000 pieces of fresh fruit, 1,500 lb lobster, 3,500 lb butter, 2,700 lb fresh vegetables and 300 cwt potatoes, along with 7,921 units of kitchen ware, 600 lbs Kosher food and 3,000 pieces Kosher crockery and 3,000 aprons for the cooks, not to mention 2,000 oven cloths and 14,000 tea towels for the waiters' and cooks' use.

For a 90 day World Cruise, the shopping list is mammoth and includes 180,000 lb beef-prime from the States, 36,000 lb lamb from Britain and 12,000 lb French veal, 11,000 lb salt, 80,000 eggs, 3 tons smoked salmon, 10 tons butter, 90,000 jars of preserve, 2,500 gallons milk and 10,000 bottles of champagne.

Things have changed since Cunard first put to sea in the 1840's. Then, on ships like the first Cunarder, the *Britannia,* the whole of which could have comfortably fitted inside the first class dining salon of the *Queen Mary,* livestock for fresh meat and a cow for milk were carried on board; though ice-houses on deck were known even as early as this. Charles Dickens, on an early crossing to the States, recalls the affection of the sailors towards the ship's cow in her little wooden house on deck. Vegetables, too, were often carried on deck and in 1854, William Chambers, of dictionary fame, noted: 'In the open space between these (the lifeboats) the cook keeps his fresh vegetables and one occasionally sees one of his assistants climbing up to clutch at a cabbage or bunch of carrots'.

Today, the QE2 has the most sophisticated of modern storage areas. There are 21 refrigerated store-rooms with variable temperatures recorded every four hours and linked to the data-logging computer of the ship. Temperatures and cleanliness are constantly monitored by Robin Davies, the QE2's hygiene officer — the first permanent appointment of this kind to be made at sea. As well as 90 food fridges in the main kitchen areas, there is an air-cooled flour/cereal store of 3,000 cubic feet, a bulk dry-goods store of 16,000 cubic feet and 27 stainless steel tanks for 313,500 gallons of draught beer. The car hold, used on transatlantic voyages, can be chilled and sectionalised and on long cruises stores some of the 120 types of wines carried. Fifty dishwashers keep the 64,000 items of crockery, 51,000 pieces of glassware and 35,850 pieces of cutlery clean; 115 vacuum cleaners and 64 carpet cleaners keep everything underfoot tidy and 240 clocks make sure everyone gets to meals on time.

Mark Twain noted an early Cunard propensity for serving stewed prunes and custard while Charles Dickens recorded his mid-Atlantic diet thus; 'At one, a bell rings and the stewardess comes down with a steaming dish of baked potatoes and another of roasted apples; and a plate of pig's face, cold ham, salt beef or perhaps a smoking mess of rare, hot collops . . . at five, another bell rings and the stewardess reappears with another dish of potatoes, boiled this time, and a store of hot meat of various kinds'.

Towards the end of the century, diners at sea were summoned to the saloon by a trumpet, sat at long tables, (glasses and wine safely stowed in racks above their heads) and sang songs between courses. Then, Captains were expected to do more than sit and chat at their table. They were expected to carve, and serve the passengers while keeping a weather eye on navigation. Thackeray, on another early Cunarder, the *Canada,* in 1852, tells this delightful Captain's Table story. 'Captain L. helped the soup with his accustomed politeness. Then he went on deck and was back in a minute and operated on the fish looking rather grave the while. Then he went on deck again and this time was absent it may be three or five minutes during which the fish disappeared and the entrées arrived and the roast beef . . . Then L. came down again with a pleased and happy countenance and began carving the sirloin. "We have seen the light", he said. "Madam, may I help you to a little gravy, or a little horseradish or what not?" I forget the name of the light, nor does it matter. It was a point of Newfoundland for which he was on the look-out and so well did *Canada* know where she was that, between the soup and the beef, the Captain had sighted the headland by which his course was lying'.

Captains of the *Queen Elizabeth 2,* with satellite navigation, computers, and the latest equipment for weather forecasting, have less need for concern when hosting their table or shaking hands with guests of their cocktail parties. Captain Robert Arnott, in his autobiography, 'Captain of the Queen', records a handshaking marathon of 635 handshakes in 34 minutes. In the 'thirties, when liners loomed larger and came complete with dining rooms that aped Roman temples or the halls of stately homes, commodores like Cunard's Sir James Charles and Sir Arthur Royston were rivals in putting on the most lavish food orgies at their tables with waiters staggering under plated plumed coveys of quail or pheasant, roast sheep and castellated puddings. Half-way across the Atlantic, those at the Captain's Table had to get the ship's tailor to let out their evening clothes. A long step forward from Dickensian days, when dishes had to be carried over open decks and puddings often arrived at table sprinkled with brine.

Though the grill rooms of the *Queen Mary* and the *Queen Elizabeth* were justly famed, it was not until the QE2 was launched in 1969 that passengers could fully indulge themselves in the traditionally lavish meals provided by Cunard. Stabilisers enable diners to keep more than their equilibrium and injections from the ship's doctor cure the queasiest of stomachs. The stabilisers, which can reduce a potential 20 degree roll to a 3 degree roll, and the use of modern, lightweight materials enabled dining rooms to be raised high up in the liner for the first time. This means that diners in the four restaurants now have sea views. The Queen's Grill, for those in the top suites, is chic and sophisticated in cobalt blue, green and silver; is decorated with Erté prints and set around a seashell sculpture lit from below. The Princess Grill is intimate in deep burgundy red, with flattering pink tablecloths, while the Columbia Restaurant is cool and airy with creamy shades and wood veneer. The largest restaurant, the Tables of the World, is divided into five sections representing different areas to which the ship cruises: Britain, Italy, France, Spain and the Orient, with decor appropriate to each — from bleached Parisian café umbrellas to oriental fans used as lightshades. The walls are decorated with Spy cartoons, John Piper and Picasso prints.

A recent addition to the ship is a spa with food ideas, from the Californian health resort, Golden Door, which daily recommends calorie-conscious menus for lunch and dinner. Healthy Golden Door soup and salad recipes are included in the new deck-buffet kitchen near the Club Lido, and with two indoor and two outdoor pools, massage, sauna, Turkish baths, yoga lessons, deck jogging and fitness tracks, gym, paddle-tennis court and golf driving range, there is no need to become unfit even while enjoying the best of the ship's food.

Certainly, hunger pangs need never be felt on the QE2. Early morning deck joggers are served coffee and buns. Breakfast can be taken in one's stateroom or more copiously in the dining rooms with everything from onion soup and lamb chops, to pickled herrings and waffles. Mid-morning coffee or bouillon is served daily; the latter being a hangover from old transatlantic days, when the steaming broth was served to those taking the sea air well cocooned in blankets in their steamer chairs. Lunch offers brunch choices for late risers; a lighter selection with soufflés for which the QE2 is famous and for which a special oven, which can cook 200 individual soufflés at one time, was installed. More recently Indian curry selections have been gaining in popularity. Because the ship is British and a lady, afternoon tea, with fresh pastries and cakes, is served in the public rooms. Then before dinner, the big and glamorous meal of the day, there are cocktail parties with caviare, canapés and other titbit temptations. On transatlantic crossings late-night snacks are served in the bars, while on cruises out of the States elaborate midnight buffets are provided in the Columbia Restaurant. If, after all that, one experiences a little night starvation, the cabin steward can fetch a drink and a sandwich.

The bakery on board works 24 hours a day, turning out anything from 300 loaves to 6,000 rolls a day, together with Danish pastries, bagels, blueberry muffins, croissants and 300 gâteaux a night for the Tables of the World Restaurant alone. Passengers are welcomed to see the open plan galley of 17,000 square feet. They can inspect the 10 gallon soup cauldrons, see 350 chickens being spit-roasted at the same time and admire the detailed work of decorating hundreds of canapés for the evening's cocktail parties.

Presiding over this never ceasing cornucopia of food production is Executive Chef, John Bainbridge. His recipes, and those of his staff, make up this book which pays tribute to their calm dedication and hard work. Born in Devon of a naval family, John Bainbridge has worked for Cunard for over 46 years with a four year break before the QE2 was launched, when he and a Cunard colleague ran a restaurant ashore. At the age of fifteen he joined the *Aquitania* as an apprentice cook and with Cunard's help, trained at the Waldorf in New York, the George V and the Ritz in Paris. In his white chef's uniform he is a familiar sight on the dockside as he and Food and Beverage Manager, Gordon Phillips, check the quality of fresh foods ordered at ports around the world. 'Soft fruits are my biggest problem,' says John Bainbridge, 'I need 1,500 avocados just to give one serving'. He knows every port by what it offers in fresh food and tries to reflect the different cuisines of places the QE2 visits on his menus. 'I love challenges,' he says; but admits that one of the most difficult requests he ever had from a passenger was to prepare fresh fish fingers for the King of Malaysia. Inspiration for more exotic foods comes from a file on his office shelf labelled, 'Recipes Rare, from Everywhere'.

Appetisers

Tomato - Grapefruit - Blended - Orange - Cranberry Juices

Chilled Honeydew Melon - Selected Caviar Glace - Salade Italienne
Hickory-Smoked Turkey Breast - Egg and Tomato, Remoulade

Soups

Chicken Gombo, Creole– *(Clear chicken with peppers, rice, tomato and okra)*
Cream of Broccoli with Croutons - Iced Beef Bouillon

From the Seas and Rivers

Appetisers

Tomato - Grapefruit - Orange - Pineapple Juices

Chilled Honeydew Melon with Proscuitto
Selected Smoked Salmon with Capers
Pate de Foie Gras, Strasbourg - Bismarck Herrings with Sour Cream

Soups

Cream of Celery - French Onion with Cheese Croutons
Chilled Gazpacho, Andaluz– *(A Spanish-style raw vegetable soup)*

Appetisers

Tomato - Grapefruit - Blended - Orange - Pineapple Juices

Chilled Honeydew Melon - Smoked Hampshire Brook Trout
Seafood Cocktail, Creole - Selected Caviar Glace
Sardines in Oil - Mousse Normande Truffe

Soups

Petite Marmite - *(A clear soup with fresh vegetables,
beef and chicken)*
Cream of Asparagus - Consommé Madrilene en Gelee

Appetisers

Tomato — Grapefruit — Orange - Pineapple Juices

Smoked Sturgeon, Chrane Sauce - Chicken Celery and Apple Salad
Chilled Melonball Cocktail, Creme de Menthe
Our Own Special Pate, Cumberland Sauce

Soups

Chiffonade
vegetable soup)

1 ATLANTIC APPETISERS, PACIFIC PREVIEWS
Soups and Starters

You can start the day on the *Queen Elizabeth 2* with **French Onion Soup** (see page 96) for breakfast, a good morning-after cure, but the ship is also renowned for its excellent soups for both lunch and dinner. They can be comforting and heart-warming after a deck walk on a brisk Atlantic day — **Yellow Pea Soup, Old Fashioned Bean Soup,** spicy **Mulligatawny** or substantial **Clam Chowder.**

Yellow Pea Soup *serves 6*

1¼ cups/10 oz/275 g yellow split peas
1 chopped onion
2 chopped sticks celery
2 chopped carrots
vegetable oil or margarine for cooking
7½ cups/3 pints/1½ litre chicken stock
salt, pepper, bay leaf

Soak peas overnight in water to cover. Place chopped vegetables in a heavy pan with oil or margarine and cook over a moderate heat with the lid on until vegetables are softened but not browned. Add drained peas, stock, salt, pepper and bay leaf and simmer for about 2 hours until the vegetables disintegrate, or put through a blender until smooth. Remove bay leaf before blending. Adjust seasoning before serving.

Old Fashioned Bean Soup
serves 6

3 cups/1 lb 2 oz/500 g navy or haricot
    beans
1 lb/½ kg piece of smoked ham or bacon
10 cups/4 pints/2 litres water
1 bay leaf
¼ tsp/1.5 ml mixed herbs
salt, pepper to taste
2 diced carrots
4 diced and peeled potatoes
4 diced celery stalks
2 large diced onions
3 oz/75 g rutabaga or yellow turnip

Soak beans overnight in boiling water to cover. Cook beans with the ham in the water with bay leaf, herbs, salt and pepper. Cook for about 2½ hours until tender. Remove meat from water and keep on one side. Add carrots, potatoes, celery, onion and rutabaga or turnip and cook for a further 1½ hours. When cooked, remove bay leaf and pass through a blender until smooth. Dice meat up when cold and use to garnish the reheated soup.

Mulligatawny Soup
serves 6

2 carrots
1 large onion
2 cooking apples
butter for cooking
bay leaf
3 tbs/45 ml curry powder
1 tb/15 ml flour
7½ cups/3 pints/1½ litres chicken stock
1 tb/15 ml orange marmalade
1 tb/15 ml desiccated coconut
1 tb/15 ml chopped sultanas
salt, pepper

A soup derived from Britain's links with India; hot and spicy for a chill day.

Chop the vegetables and apples and simmer in the butter in a big pan with the lid on until softened but not coloured. Add bay leaf, flour and curry powder and mix to form a roux. Add chicken stock, stir well until blended and smooth. Add marmalade, coconut, sultanas and seasoning to taste. Heat gently until the mixture thickens, stirring well all the time. Lower heat and simmer for about an hour. Adjust thickness of the soup with more stock if necessary and remove bay leaf. Strain soup or pass through a blender. Cream can be blended into the soup if a richer finish is required and about 2 oz/50 g diced cooked chicken and 3 oz/75 g cooked rice can also be added, if wished, as a garnish.

Clam Chowder
serves 4–6

20 clams (fresh or canned)
3 oz/75 g diced salt pork   *(continued)*

Boil or steam the clams (if fresh) for 10 minutes. Remove membrane and chop. Cook clams with pork

18

2 large sliced onions
1 large sliced leek
1 peeled and chopped tomato
7 oz/200 g canned tomatoes
1 diced stick celery
½ tb/7 ml chopped parsley
½ tsp/2.5 ml thyme
1 small bay leaf
1 large diced potato
dash Worcester sauce
dash Tabasco sauce
salt, pepper
butter for cooking

until golden in a little butter, add onions, tomatoes, leeks and celery and seasonings to taste. Measure the amount of broth in the pan and make up to 3 cups plus 2 tbs/1¼ pints/725 ml with water. Cook for 40 minutes adding potato, Worcester sauce and Tabasco. Remove bay leaf and check seasoning before serving.

Potage Elizabeth Jubilee *serves 5*

A creamy chicken-and-leek based soup devised for the Jubilee year of 1977, in honour of Her Majesty who launched the ship in 1969. The soup is garnished with diced chicken, York ham, asparagus tips and strips of leek.

3 large leeks
butter for cooking
2 tbs/30 ml flour
3 cups plus 2 tbs/1¼ pints/725 ml
    chicken stock (made using leeks
    instead of onion in the flavouring)
salt, freshly ground black pepper
½ cup plus 2 tbs/¼ pint/150 ml light
    (single) cream
to garnish:
1 oz/25 g diced white cooked chicken
½ oz/13 g diced York ham
1 chopped asparagus tip
1 small leek, cooked and cut in fine strips

Dice the white sections of the leeks and cook slowly in butter until soft but not browned. Stir in flour and cook slowly. Remove from heat and add the chicken stock and seasoning and bring to the boil, stirring constantly until thickened. Lower heat and simmer for one hour. Allow to cool and pass through a fine sieve or blender. Add the cream and season to taste, reheat and serve garnished with a little of the chicken, ham, asparagus and leek on each serving.

In contrast, after a hot and sticky sightseeing day ashore in the Caribbean or Pacific ports, cold soups provide a throat-soothing start to a meal. In the two grill rooms, cold soups are served in scallop-shaped plated dishes nestled in snow-ice. A favourite for parched throats is this simple, but superb tasting, **Ananas Kaltschale,** an unusual blend of white wine and fruit juice.

Ananas Kaltschale *serves 4*

1 small can crushed pineapple
1 small can pineapple juice
½ cup plus 2 tbs/¼ pint/150 ml cream (thin)
½ cup plus 2 tbs/¼ pint/150 ml white wine

Blend together pineapple and pineapple juice and add cream and white wine mixing until smooth and chill well before serving. Do not make too long in advance of serving.

One of my own favourite QE2 soups is the classic American soup, **Crème Vichyssoise;** smooth and soothing.

Crème Vichyssoise *serves 4*

2 leeks
1 small onion
1 tb/15 ml butter
2–3 medium sized potatoes
2½ cups/1 pint/575 ml chicken stock
½ tb/7 ml salt
1¼ cups/½ pint/275 ml milk
1¼ cups/½ pint/275 ml medium thick cream
salt, fresh ground black pepper
½ cup plus 2 tbs/¼ pint/150 ml heavy (double) cream
finely chopped chives

Slice finely the white parts of the leeks, slice the onion and cook together in the butter until golden and softened. Add peeled and chopped potatoes, chicken stock and salt, and simmer gently for about 40 minutes. Rub through a fine sieve or blend. Return to the heat and add milk, cream (medium), season to taste and bring to the boil. Allow to cool and when cold add the heavy (double) cream and serve sprinkled with finely chopped chives.

John Bainbridge, Executive Chef (second left), shares a joke with some of his colleagues.

Chilled Cream of Cucumber Soup *serves 4*

2 cucumbers
1 onion
¼ cup/2 oz/50 g butter
⅛ cup/½ oz/13 g flour
1¾ cup/14 fl oz/400 ml chicken stock
salt, pepper to taste
1 cup minus 1 tb/7 fl oz/200 ml light
     (single) cream
juice of 1 lemon
sprig of mint

Peel cucumbers and dice finely. Cook with diced onion in the butter until softened but do not allow to brown. Add flour and stir for a few minutes. Remove from the heat and add preheated chicken stock. Season to taste and cook gently, stirring occasionally, for 45 minutes. Pass through a fine sieve or blender and when cold, add cream and lemon juice. Serve well chilled with a sprinkling of chopped mint.

Originating in Spain, and another perfect hot-weather soup is **Gazpacho.** Cunard have their own well established version that makes a good slimming starter.

Cunard Gazpacho

serves 6–8

3 x 14 oz/400 ml cans tomato juice
2 x 14 oz/400 ml cans V8 juice
1 lb/450 g peeled, seeded and finely
    chopped tomatoes
¼ cup/2 oz/50 g finely chopped green
    pepper
½ cup/4 oz/125 g finely chopped onions
1 oz/25 g finely chopped beetroot
½ oz/13 g finely chopped parsley
juice of 1 lemon
pinch of tarragon
a few chopped chives
salt, freshly ground black pepper
½ cup + 2 tbs/¼ pint/150 ml olive oil
3 tbs/45 ml white wine vinegar
1 crushed clove of garlic
8 oz/225 g diced cucumber

Mix all the ingredients together, with the exception of the cucumber, in a large bowl. Chill for at least 2 hours and add the cucumber just before serving and serve with a side dish of croûtons (fried cubes of bread) as a garnish.

Recipes from the 'Golden Door Cookery Book' by spa owner Deborah Szekely and her chef Michel Stroot, who have both travelled on the QE2, are healthy and summery. One of their soup and salad combinations served from the new Club Lido deck-kitchen and buffet servery is a conscience-clear lunch for those who keep in trim at the six deck spa's exercise and dance programmes, or follow Eric Mason's easy yoga classes. Eric, an ex-RAF physical training instructor, reckons he can teach anyone of any age eight basic yoga positions even on a five day transatlantic crossing.

The Golden Door believes in lots of fresh fruit and the advice, freely given to all passengers on the QE2, was so effective on the 1983 Pacific Cruise that in five days 1,200 lb of bananas were eaten and the chef had to telex Cartagena and Acapulco for more supplies to be boarded.

Golden Door Grapefruit Gazpacho *serves 4*

2 medium tomatoes, peeled, seeded and
    finely chopped
1 cup/8 oz/225 g peeled and grated
    cucumber
½ cup/4 oz/125 g finely chopped celery
½ cup/4 oz/125 g finely chopped
    peppers
2 tbs/30ml chopped fresh parsley
1½ cups/12 fl oz/350 ml fresh
    grapefruit juice
parsley to garnish

Combine all the ingredients by hand or in the pulse cycle of a blender. Chill for at least two hours and garnish with parsley before serving.

Mushroom Salad (cold or warm) *serves 4*

1½ tbs/22 ml sun-dried white raisins
1 tb/15 ml minced shallots or scallions
    (spring onions)
1 tsp/5 ml minced garlic
2 tbs/30 ml olive oil
1 lb/½ kg fresh mushrooms
1 tsp/5 ml dried whole thyme or ½ tsp/
    2.5 ml fresh thyme
1 tsp/5 ml vegetable seasoning
½ tsp/2.5 ml freshly ground black
    pepper
¼ cup/2 fl oz/50 ml dry white wine
1 cup/8 oz/225 g peeled, seeded and
    diced tomato
1 tb/15 ml fresh lemon juice
¼ cup/2 oz/50 g chopped fresh parsley
lettuce leaves for garnish

Pre-soak raisins in warm water to cover until plumped up. In a heavy pan, gently fry shallots with garlic in 1 tb/15 ml olive oil until they start to soften. Add mushrooms, thyme, vegetable seasoning, and pepper. Stir with a wooden spatula. Quickly add wine, tomato, raisins (drained), and lemon juice. Remove from heat as soon as the mixture comes to the boil. Sprinkle with parsley and the remainder of the olive oil. Serve warm or cold.

Green Salad with Onion and Orange *serves 4*

1 halved clove of garlic
3 cups/1½ lbs/¾ kg watercress sprigs or
   small pieces of curly endive or
   romaine lettuce
2 slices onion of the sweet, white or red
   variety separated into rings, or 2
   thinly sliced green onions
1 orange, small and peeled, seeded and
   thinly sliced
1 tb/15 ml corn or olive oil
1 tsp/5 ml red wine vinegar
1 tsp/5 ml red wine (or water)
pinch dry mustard powder
sea salt to taste, freshly ground black
   pepper

Rub salad bowl with the cut side of garlic. Add greens, onions and orange. Mix the rest of the ingredients in a blender and then scatter over the watercress and toss with a fork. Add more vinegar as needed and serve at once.

The *Queen Elizabeth 2* is the world's biggest single buyer of caviare. Only the best Beluga and Sevruga are carried and imitations like lump fish roe are nowhere to be seen on the canapés or other dishes. Further details and recipes are given in later chapters but those who want to make caviare go a little further, or try a substitute presentation for **Salmon à la Russe,** can copy an idea from David Calder, Head Waiter in the Queen's Grill. David Calder's grand-father was 46 years with Cunard and David's first association with the company was as a small child helping grandfather clean the brass port-holes of the *Queen Mary* in Southampton docks.

For **Salmon à la Russe,** slices of smoked salmon are rolled into small cornets, filled with caviare and presented on cucumber and hard-boiled egg slices decorated with tiny, thin lemon fans. David, however, recalls a smoked salmon recipe, devised for a Texan couple, that makes a less expensive but

Opposite:
Beluga caviare. The ship is the world's biggest single buyer.

refreshing meal starter. Spinach, cooked with a little salt and nutmeg, is strained and dried as much as possible then mixed with sour cream and chilled in the fridge until firm. The mixture is then used as a very effective filling for slices of rolled smoked salmon.

A more elaborate hors d' œuvre, which has been demonstrated by Chef Bainbridge on American TV, has artichoke bottoms stuffed with chicken liver paté and onions, cooked in sherry and covered with a tarragon flavoured Hollandaise Sauce.

Avocados are widely used on the ship, especially on cruises, and keeping an adequate supply of ripe ones while at sea is a chef's headache. A simple but excellent and very refreshing flavour-combination salad served at lunchtime, is thinly sliced avocado with tinned grapefruit segments garnished with lettuce. **Avocado Royale** consists of avocado flesh scooped from the shell and mixed with flaked crab-meat and bound with a Thousand Island dressing. A thin layer of dressing is added to cover the mixture in the shell before serving on coloured snow-ice or in a folded napkin.

Another avocado idea is named after Acapulco; a well liked port of call on World Cruises. (After all the Mexicans did first grow the avocado.)

Acapulco Delight
serves 4

3 very ripe avocado pears
juice of 1 lemon
salt, pepper
1 crushed clove of garlic
pinch chili powder
¼ cup/2 oz/50 g finely diced Spanish onion
⅛ cup/1 oz/25 g finely diced green pepper
6 oz/175 g tiny shrimp
sliced stuffed olives for garnish

Remove flesh from avocado shells and keep four of the half-shells. Sieve flesh and beat well with lemon juice, seasoning, garlic and chili powder. Add onion and peppers. Line the inside of the pear shells with tiny shrimp and spoon the avocado mixture back into the shells. Decorate with sliced, stuffed olives on top and a few shrimps. Serve with lettuce leaves and tomato wedges.

On the ship, recipes are often named after the passenger to whom they were first served. This easy, but delicious hors d'œuvre was named after a certain passenger called Pedro.

Pear Pedro

serves 1

½ ripe pear
juice of 1 lemon
¼ cup/1½ oz/37 g Philadelphia cream
    cheese
½ oz/12 g diced green peppers
1 tsp/5 ml chopped chives
for dressing:
6 oz/175 ml yoghurt
2 tbs/30 ml chopped parsley
pinch of tarragon
Romaine lettuce to serve

Peel, core and cut pear in half lengthways. Brush with lemon juice. Prepare filling mixture, blending together cream cheese, peppers, and chives. Pipe or mound onto the centre of the pear. Coat with a dressing made from the yoghurt mixed with parsley and tarragon and arrange pear on lettuce leaves.

Jumbo-sized shrimps are used on the ship for hors d'œuvres and canapé ideas. This recipe makes use of Dublin Bay style prawns and, in the restaurants of the QE2, is prepared at the tableside and flamed in cognac.

Shrimp Baratin

serves 4

¼ cup plus ½ tb/2½ oz/62 g butter
3 dozen medium-sized raw shrimp or
    prawns, shelled and de-veined
salt, freshly ground black pepper
2 tbs/3 ml finely minced shallots
1 tsp/5 ml lemon juice
3 tbs/45 ml warmed brandy

Melt the butter in a large pan and when hot add the shrimp. Sprinkle evenly with salt and pepper. Cook until pink on both sides — about 4 minutes. Sprinkle the shrimp with shallots, lemon juice and continue to cook and stir. Sprinkle the warmed brandy over the shrimp and flame. Spoon the sauce over and over the shrimp as the flame burns. Serve at once as an appetiser.

2 FRUITS DE MER
Main Course
Fish Dishes

With over 67,000 tons cutting through the ocean at a service speed of 28½ knots it's hard to imagine fish being able to stop such a powerful lady in her ocean tracks. But on one occasion in the Bahamas, humble jelly-fish ganged up in thousands to clog her movement very effectively. On another occasion, in mid-Atlantic, the bow hit a dead whale floating on the surface. The whale stuck right across the bows and the whole ship shuddered for several hours until both ends of the whale were eventually shaken free.

Fish for the table can be a problem too; deciding the amounts needed fresh in each port is quite a task. Seven hundred pounds are needed for just one serving. In New York for one cruise 35,000 dollars were spent on crabmeat enough for one dish for everyone on board. Lobster is one of the seafoods most frequently featured on the ship's menus but even for one serving, 15,000 lb are needed. The lobsters come on board live and are prepared for the table by the larder cooks; not one of their favourite tasks. Ted Vamplew, from Southampton, says his hands swell from the water after splitting 1,800 lobsters at a session. Starting at 7 am, 900 lobsters are split, and the claws cracked, by 9.30 am, ready for the lunchtime serving cold with mayonnaise. Each diner gets a half lobster and the whole coral is kept for serving **Lobster Américaine.**

The QE2 once enjoyed the unusual treat of eating vegetarian lobsters. This was in Tristan da Cunha on the 1979 World Cruise, where the ship's visit to a community smaller than itself, a self-sufficient and isolated island, was commemorated in special stamps. The Tristan lobsters, far from any human pollution, live on seaweed on the shelving rocks around the island and were very sweet and tender.

Among the many ways the ship serves lobster are the following:

Creamed Lobster   *serves 3–4*

Can be served as an hors d'œuvre or with rice as a main course.

1 lb/450 g lobster meat
¼ cup/2 oz/50 g butter
2 shallots
2 tsp/10 ml sherry
paprika, salt
2 egg yolks
6 tbs/90 ml cream
a little finely chopped parsley or chives

Dice lobster and toss in melted butter with minced shallot for 2 minutes. Add sherry, paprika, and salt to taste. Blend in beaten egg yolks and cream, and stir the lobster into this sauce over a gentle heat. Take care not to let the mixture boil. Serve at once sprinkled with a little chopped parsley or chives.

Shrimp and Lobster Jamboli   *serves 4*

1 oz/25 g butter
pinch mixed herbs or oregano
1 finely minced clove of garlic
1 oz/25 g sliced green peppers
¼ cup/2 oz/50 g sliced tomatoes
¼ cup/1 oz/25 g sliced onions
1 oz/25 g shredded cabbage   *(continued)*

Melt a little butter in a pan and cook herbs, garlic, peppers, tomatoes, onions and cabbage until softened but not browned. Add the lobster and flamed shrimps or prawns and cook gently through. Season to taste. Serve with cooked, long-grain, white rice.

8 oz/225 g diced, cooked lobster
8 oz/225 g whole shrimps or prawns
  which have been flamed in brandy
salt, a little freshly ground black pepper

Crayfish Tail Princess

serves 4

A dish named after the Princess Grill on the ship; the original Grill Room shaded in burgundy-reds with big picture windows looking out on the sea.

4 cloves of garlic
⅓ cup/2 oz/50 g chopped onion
¼ cup/2 oz/50 g chopped celery
⅛ cup/1 oz/25 g chopped green peppers
¼ cup/2 oz/50 g chopped red peppers
4 oz/125 g peeled tomatoes
1 oz/25 g chopped parsley
½ cup/4 fl oz/125 ml white wine
1 tsp/5 ml arrowroot or cornstarch
  (cornflour)
1 lb/450 g cooked crayfish tail meat or
  lobster
1 cup/ 8 oz/225 g cooked long-grain rice
salt, freshly ground black pepper

Simmer all the ingredients (except the wine, rice and fish) together in the butter, cooking through gently without browning. Add white wine and bring mixture to the boil. Thicken with 1 tsp/5 ml arrowroot or cornstarch (cornflour) and season to taste. Dice crayfish or lobster and add to the sauce. Serve with cooked rice.

Fruits de Mer Caprice

serves 6–8

¾ lb/350 g lobster meat
16 medium-sized shrimps, peeled and
  de-veined
salt, freshly ground black pepper
2½ oz/62 g butter
12 oz/350 g scallops
2 tbs/30 ml finely chopped shallots
10 oz/275 g sliced mushrooms
1½ cups/12 fl oz/350 ml heavy
  (double) cream
2 egg yolks
1 tsp/5 ml lemon juice
cayenne pepper, or Tabasco sauce

Dice lobster meat and sprinkle the shrimps with salt and pepper. Heat half the butter in a pan and add the shrimps, cooking quickly. Remove with a slotted spoon and keep hot. Melt the remaining butter in the same pan and add the scallops. Cook briefly, barely cooking through, tossing and stirring the fish for about one minute. Add shallots, mushrooms, shrimps and the diced lobster and cook for about a further minute, tossing and stirring all the time. Remove seafood with a slotted spoon and keep warm. Reduce the liquid in the pan to about half its original amount and add 1¼ cups/½ pint/275 ml cream and simmer for about 10 minutes. Combine the egg yolks with the rest of the cream and add to the hot sauce off the heat. Add lemon juice and cayenne or Tabasco sauce to taste and return to the heat. Bring almost to the boil, stirring constantly. Add seafood and continue cooking and stirring until just thick. Do not cook over a high heat or the eggs may curdle the sauce. Serve with rice. The dish can also be served in gratin dishes as an appetiser.

Seafood Crêpes
serves 8–10

16 crêpes made with fine herb flavouring
   (for crêpe mix see page 64)
1½ cups plus 2 tbs/¾ pint/425 ml
   Curry Sauce (see below)
butter for cooking
2 tbs/30 ml finely chopped shallots
½ cup/4 fl oz/125 ml dry white wine
1 tb/15 ml each of finely chopped chives,
   parsley and tarragon
10 oz/275 g finely chopped, cooked
   lobster
10 oz/275 g finely chopped, cooked
   shrimps or prawns
10 oz/275 g finely chopped, cooked
   crabmeat
salt, freshly ground black pepper

Make crêpes (see page 64) and make the **Curry Sauce** (see below). While the sauce is simmering, prepare the crêpe filling by placing 3 tbs/45 ml butter in a pan. Add shallots and cook briefly, stirring, and then add the wine. Cook until the liquid is reduced by half. Add herbs and seafood and stir to blend. Sprinkle with salt and pepper to taste and cook briefly, stirring, until heated through. Spoon portions of the mixture into the centre of each crêpe and roll up. Arrange crêpes on a platter and brush them with melted butter. Butter a sheet of greaseproof paper and place it, buttered side down, over the crêpes. Cover and place in the oven. Cook for a little while in a low oven until just heated through but not until really piping hot. Serve on hot plates with the **Curry Sauce.**

Curry Sauce
makes about 2 cups/¾ pint/425 ml

4½ tbs/67 ml butter
1 finely minced clove of garlic
½ cup/3 oz/75 g finely chopped onion
⅓ cup/3 oz/75 g finely chopped celery
3 tbs/45 ml chopped carrot
2 tbs/30 ml flour
2 tbs/30 ml curry powder
1 bay leaf   (continued)

Heat 3 tbs/45 ml of the butter in a pan and add garlic, onion, celery and carrot. Cook, stirring, until onion is softened but not browned. Add the flour and cook, stirring, for about 3 minutes. Stir in the curry powder, bay leaf, parsley and thyme. Use a wire whisk, stir briskly while adding the chicken stock. Simmer covered, stirring occasionally, for about 30

The QE2 at night, when the restaurants are busiest.

2 sprigs parsley
2 sprigs fresh thyme or ½ tsp/2.5 ml
  dried thyme
2 cups/16 fl oz/450 ml chicken stock
salt, freshly ground black pepper

minutes. Remove the bay leaf and pass the mixture through a fine sieve or put through the blender. Swirl the remaining butter round the pan juices, add salt and pepper to taste and add to the sauce.

Chef Derrick Leigh created the following de luxe lobster recipe for one of his passengers during the 1979 World Cruise and named it after her. Derrick Leigh, from Southampton, first joined Cunard in 1950 as a kitchen porter on the *Mauretania* and was a chef on the *Queen Elizabeth* for nine years before joining the QE2. Another of Derrick Leigh's culinary inventions which can be copied for a dinner party, is **Caravan Crêpes.** Cook seafood, or white fish which will hold its shape until smooth, with sherry, chopped mushrooms and seasoning in butter. Add a little flour, stir until mixed and add cream, stirring to make a thick, smooth sauce. Fold crêpes (see page 64) in envelope shape round the fish filling. Brush with beaten egg and dip in breadcrumbs. Deep- or shallow-fry in butter and serve with a sherry and mushroom sauce. Derrick's tip is to brush the crêpes twice with butter before adding the filling and to freeze for fifteen minutes before frying.

Lobster Gloria F   *serves 6*

6 x 1 lb/450 g cooked lobsters, split in
  half
½ cup plus 2 tbs/¼ pint/150 ml sherry
½ cup plus 2 tbs/¼ pint/150 ml white
  wine
1 small diced red pepper
4 large tomatoes, skinned, de-seeded and
  diced
1 whole chopped truffle (optional, as
  very expensive)
12 green parts of spring onions, chopped

(continued)

Split lobsters, remove meat and dice. Reserve shells. Add to a pan, the sherry, white wine, pepper, tarragon, truffle (if used), tomatoes, and onions, and season to taste. Boil to reduce the amount of liquid by one third. Add lobster meat and shrimps and simmer until most of the liquid has been absorbed. Add cream, stir and simmer until mixture thickens. Spoon mixture into the lobster shells and serve with the sauce and garnish with watercress.

salt, freshly ground black pepper
8 oz/225 g shelled and de-veined
    shrimps or prawns
½ cup plus 2 tbs/¼ pint/150ml heavy
    (double) cream
watercress to garnish
for sauce:
4 oz/125 g shrimps or prawns
½ cup plus 2 tbs/¼ pint/150 ml sherry
1 tb/15 ml Dijon mustard
4 egg yolks
½ cup plus 2 tbs/¼ pint/150 ml cream

To make sauce: place shrimps, mustard and sherry in a pan and reduce to a third of the quantity. Blend egg yolks with the cream and add to the pan, stir quickly and take care that the mixture does not boil and curdle. When thickened, spoon over the lobsters.

With the ship's passion for flambéing foods, creating a little drama in the dining rooms and adding flavour — without too much alcohol — to the food, **Scampi au Pernod** is a well established special order recipe in the Columbia Restaurant and makes an easy dish for a dinner party or even a barbecue party.

Scampi au Pernod   *serves 4*

½ oz/12 g butter
½ cup/4 oz/125 g chopped tomatoes
1 chopped clove of garlic
¼ cup/2 oz/50 g chopped red and green
    peppers
about 16 scampi
1 measure Pernod

Melt butter and add tomatoes, garlic and peppers. Cook until softened but not browned. Meanwhile grill the scampi threaded on skewers, kebab style. Remove scampi from the skewers and place in a pan with the sauce. Reduce the sauce in the pan until thick and heat 1 measure Pernod in a small pan. Flame this and pour over the scampi. Serve with boiled rice.

Shrimps Inverrary   *serves 4*

¼ cup/2 oz/50 g diced shallots or onions
2 oz/50 g sliced mushrooms
butter to cook
2½ cups/1 pint/575 ml light (single)
    cream
1 tsp/5 ml cornstarch (cornflour)

A dish created by Chef Bainbridge when the Duke of Argyll, head of the Clan Campbell, dined on board to launch the exclusive twelve-year-old QE2 malt whisky sold on the ship, which is produced at Campbelltown on the Argyll estate.

(continued)

This solid silver pot was presented
to Samuel Cunard, founder of the line,
in 1840.

2 egg yolks
½ cup/4 oz/125 ml malt whisky
2½ cups/20 oz/575 g cooked shrimps
(either the American or smaller
British prawns)
salt, freshly ground black pepper

Fry onions and mushrooms gently in the butter and add the cream. Cook until the liquid is reduced and thicken slightly with cornstarch dissolved in a little water. Remove from the heat and add 2 egg yolks making sure that the mixture does not boil. Add whisky and mix in. Pour sauce over the shrimps and season with salt and pepper. Serve with boiled rice.

Devilled Crab

serves 6

4 tbs/60 ml butter
1 tb/15 ml vegetable oil
¾ cup/6 oz/175 g minced onion
½ cup/4 oz/125 g chopped celery
3 tbs/45 ml flour
1½ cups/12 fl oz/350 ml milk
1 cup/8 fl oz/225 ml light (single) cream
1½ tsps/7.5 ml dry mustard
few drops Tabasco sauce
1 tsp/5 ml Worcester sauce
¼ cup/2 fl oz/50 ml dry sherry
2 tbs/30 ml fresh lemon juice
2 tbs/50 ml chopped parsley
3 hard-boiled eggs
1 lb/450 g flaked fresh crabmeat
salt and white pepper to taste
½ cup/4½ oz/137 g grated Parmesan
cheese

In a large frying pan, mix 3 tbs/45 ml of the butter with the oil and fry the onion and celery over a low heat for 4–6 minutes or until soft. Add the flour a little at a time and cook, stirring, for 3–4 minutes. Meanwhile heat the milk and cream in a small pan and add the heated milk gradually to the onion mixture, stirring constantly. In a small bowl mix mustard, Tabasco, Worcester sauce, sherry, lemon juice and parsley. Add this to the onion mixture in the pan, stirring well. Bring to the simmer and stir until the sauce thickens, about 3–4 minutes. Add the chopped eggs and crab meat. Check seasoning, adding salt and pepper to taste. Divide mixture among 6 scallop shells or ramekin dishes. Dot the top with the remaining butter and cover with the cheese. Place in a preheated oven at 375F/190C/Gas 5 for 15 minutes or until the tops are lightly browned and bubbling.

Sole is a fish which shows its versatility on the ship. Dressed up in dinner finery it is **Dover Sole Caprice** with **Sauce Robert;** and one of Chef Bainbridge's personal favourites. Elegant, but lighter, is John Bainbridge's **Quenelles of Sole Ryst.** Or, light and simple for a quick dinner dish, is David Calder's **Sole Countess** which he makes for those dining in the Queen's Grill who want something light and easy on the digestion.

Fillet of Dover Sole Caprice

serves 4

8 fillets Dover sole
flour for coating
1 cup/8 oz/225 g unsalted butter
2 cups/8 oz/225 g fresh white
    breadcrumbs
4 bananas

Melt the butter and dust the fillets of sole with flour, dip into the melted butter and then finally coat with the breadcrumbs. Place under the grill and cook until golden brown, turning occasionally. Slice bananas lengthways, one for every two fillets and very lightly fry in a little butter and place on the sole fillets. Serve with **Sauce Robert** (see below).

Sauce Robert

2 medium onions, chopped
2 chopped cloves of garlic
¼ cup/2 oz/50 g butter
1¼ cups/½ pint/275 ml white wine
2 tbs/30 ml malt vinegar
1 tb/15 ml brown sugar
1 tb/15 ml redcurrant jelly
½ cup plus 2 tbs/¼ pint/150 ml tomato
    ketchup
1 tsp/5 ml cornstarch (cornflour)
1 tb/15 ml dry mustard
1 tsp/5 ml Worcester sauce
¼ cup/2 oz/50 g butter

Melt butter in a pan and add onions and garlic and simmer until cooked but do not allow to brown. When softened, add white wine, vinegar, brown sugar and redcurrant jelly and cook until sauce is reduced by half. Add tomato ketchup and thicken with cornstarch dissolved in a little water, and bring to the boil, stirring well. Mix mustard with Worcester sauce and blend into the sauce. Remove from the heat, add butter and stir well in to give a glossy finish.

Quenelles of Sole Ryst

serves 4

1 lb/450 g fillets of sole
½ cup/4 fl oz/125 ml milk
½ cup/4 oz/125 g butter
½ cup/4 oz/125 ml water
2 cups/8 oz/225 g flour
¼ tsp/1.5 ml salt
pinch pepper and nutmeg
3 egg yolks
3 egg whites
Court-bouillon made from:
2½ cups/1 pint/575 ml water in which
    herbs, sliced carrot, onion and bay
    leaf have been cooked for 30 minutes
    and then strained.   *(continued)*

Mince sole and put in a blender until smooth. Leave on one side. Make a choux paste by bringing milk, butter and water to the boil together. Stir in the flour and cook, stirring, until the mixture leaves the sides of the pan. Remove from the heat and add salt, pepper, nutmeg and beat in the egg yolks. Beat in the fish and whisk the egg whites until stiff. Fold into the fish mixture. Shape the mixture into egg shapes using two spoons and slip the pieces of fish into the simmering Court-bouillon. Simmer for 30 minutes; drain fish from the liquid and place in an ovenproof dish and keep warm.

for White Wine Sauce:
1¼ cups/½ pint/275 ml heavy (double)
 cream
1¼ cups/½ pint/275 ml light (single)
 cream
1¼ cups/½ pint/275 ml white wine
½ tb/7 ml cornstarch (cornflour)
2 egg yolks

To make the sauce: boil the remaining poaching liquid until greatly reduced and then add it to the cream and white wine and allow to simmer, thickening slightly with cornstarch dissolved in a little water. Remove from the heat and finish by adding 2 egg yolks, making sure that the mixture does not reboil. Pour the sauce over the fish quenelles and place dish under the grill for a few minutes to brown.

Sole Countess   *serves 4*

8 sole fillets
butter to cook
salt, freshly ground black pepper
1 glass dry white wine
1 lemon
4 oz/125 g cooked, drained spinach
a little thick cream
chopped parsley

Melt butter in a pan and fry the fish on a low heat with salt, pepper, turning fillets to cook evenly for about 3–4 minutes. Remove the fish from the pan and keep hot on a serving plate. Add the wine and lemon juice to the butter in the pan and swirl it around the pan to make a light, clean sauce for the fish. Garnish with a little chopped parsley on the fish and serve with spinach, flavoured with nutmeg and mixed with a little cream, and small potatoes.

Pastas appear on the menus everyday and a sauce which goes well with virtually any pasta, particularly rigatoni, spaghetti or noodles, is **Red Clam Sauce.**

Red Clam Sauce   *serves 4*

4 tbs/60 ml olive oil
4 skinned, de-seeded tomatoes, chopped
 finely
2 large minced onions
4 minced cloves of garlic
¼ tsp/1.5 ml oregano
¼ tsp/1.5 ml mixed herbs
¼ tsp/1.5 tomato purée
10 oz/275 g minced clams
salt, freshly ground black pepper
1 tb/15 ml chopped parsley

Lightly cook tomatoes, onions, and garlic with the herbs in the olive oil until vegetables are softened but not browned. Add tomato purée and minced clams, season to taste and gently simmer until cooked. Finish by stirring in the parsley and serve with any pasta dish.

3 CORDON BLEU TO COTTAGE PIE
Meat and Poultry Main Dishes

The QE2's Restaurant Managers, like David Chambers of the Princess Grill, have noticed lighter eating patterns over the past couple of years with passengers cutting down on breakfast — going more for Continental amounts — and eating more cheese soufflés and salads at lunch. However, the ship's evening meal, with its main meat course, is not going out of fashion as *the* meal of the day.

Special dishes and gala-night menus are described in the following chapter, but Cunard is lavish with its everyday meat portions; with huge steaks, racks of lamb or pork loin. One World Cruise passenger liked his dinner-time **Roast Loin of Pork** so much he asked for a doggy bag so he could take the left overs to his suite for a midnight snack sitting on his balcony watching the Caribbean flow past.

He could have taken it, of course, to the dog kennel deck aloft and shared it with the canine passengers. There's usually only a poodle or two on a long cruise but the QE2 employs two kennel maids and carries 50 lb of dog biscuits on every transatlantic crossing. The dog deck has everything a pampered travelling pet could need, with room to stroll and a London lamppost for ablutions. Cats and parrots are often carried and a Great Dane has been the largest animal aboard. One transatlantic passenger took her pet birds in her cabin with her, and the ship's manifest sheet at every port lists 'one budgie remaining on board'. It belongs to the bosun. When the ship gets to South American ports there is usually a crew urge to buy a parrot. There is the story of Sammy, a big parrot who loved life at sea until he flew into the ship's Christmas tree, fused the lights and blew all his feathers off. Then there were the two waiters who went ashore to buy a parrot. Not speaking the local language they made wing-flapping signs to a taxi driver who took them, not to a pet shop, but to the airport, some way out of town and the two missed sailing time and paid the penalty for their parrot; an expensive bird.

Stories like these enliven cocktail conversation before dinner. While the bringing of livestock on board involves port health formalities, not all passengers believe there will be enough lavish food in mid-ocean. Actress Frances Day, on the maiden voyage of the *Queen Mary,* took live chickens with her because she did not think Cunard capable of providing fresh eggs mid-Atlantic. A more recent passenger took his own supply of poultry and game birds. He was in the poultry business and believed his birds were the best. Another passenger ordered partridge seven times so he could get it just the way he liked it at home; half steamed, half roasted.

But passengers need never worry about a shortage of meat or poultry on board; 5,000 lb of chicken alone are carried on each transatlantic voyage.

Veal is one of the most popular meats used on board the QE2 and there are many recipes using the delicate meat. The classic Cordon Bleu recipe is made by sandwiching thin veal escalopes with Westphalian ham and Mozzarella cheese slices with a sprinkle of oregano, breadcrumbed and fried and served with a tomato, shallot and garlic sauce garnish.

The veal used is French and it comes on board in

30 lb legs and when the ship is full, 22 legs a night have to be boned out by the larder chefs ready for cooking. One recipe liked by passengers is **Escalope of Veal Orloff QE2,** a variation of the classic dish.

Escalope of Veal Orloff QE2 *serves 4*

4 x 1 in/2½ cm veal escalopes
butter for cooking
6 oz/175 g calf's liver
1 tb/15 ml sherry
chicken stock to cover
½ cup minus 1 tb/3 oz/75 g rice
3 oz/75 g onions
3 oz/75 g mushrooms
salt, pepper
chopped parsley

for Cheese Sauce:
1¼ cups/½ pint/275 ml milk
1 tb/15 ml butter
½ cup/2 oz/50 g flour
1½ cups/6 oz/175 g cheese, preferably
Parmesan

Flatten out the veal escalopes with a meat mallet. Cook veal quickly in butter and keep hot. Make a paste by cooking the calf's liver gently with the diced onions. Add the sherry. After cooking until tender, chop finely, and spread the paste over the escalopes. Boil the rice, chopped onions and sliced mushrooms in the chicken stock to cover. When rice is cooked, place in a blender until a paste is formed and spread this over the top of the other paste on the meat. Finally, cover the escalopes with a cheese sauce made by melting the butter in a pan, mixing in the flour, and blending in milk. Stir until thickened and season with salt and pepper to taste and adding in the cheese until smooth.

Escalope of Veal Derico *serves 4*

An interesting blend of veal, and spinach and mushrooms, with avocado and named after the chefs in the galley.

½ cup/4 oz/124 g sliced mushrooms
1 sliced green pepper
butter to cook
¾ cup/6 oz/175 g chopped spinach
¼ cup/2 fl oz/50 ml sherry
¾ cup/6 oz/175 ml cream sauce (made
from chicken stock, thickened with 1
tsp/5 ml cornstarch (cornflour)
blended in a little water and mixed in
until thick with cream) *(continued)*

Cook mushrooms and green pepper in butter until softened but not browned. Add chopped, cooked spinach, and sherry. Blend with the cream sauce, season to taste and fold in the avocado flesh. Spoon about 4 oz/125 g of the mixture onto a slice of the veal which has been well flattened with a meat mallet and cover with another slice of veal, tucking the edges in envelope style to contain the filling. Dust with flour,

nutmeg, oregano, salt, pepper to taste
1 diced avocado pear
8 x 3 oz/75 g thin flattened pieces of
    veal
beaten egg
flour to coat
breadcumbs
butter to cook

beaten egg and breadcrumbs twice. Shallow-fry in butter and serve with a cream sauce made as above flavoured with the juice of 2 lemons.

Veal and Waterchestnuts   serves 6

2 lbs/1 kg boneless veal, cut in small
    pieces as for a stew
½ cup/4 oz/125 g butter
1 crushed clove of garlic
1 medium grated onion
1 lb/575 g sliced mushrooms
10 oz/275 g can of beef bouillon
pinch nutmeg
1 bay leaf
salt, pepper
1 large can sliced waterchestnuts
1 cup/8 oz/225 ml heavy (double) cream
chopped parsley

Preheat the oven to 375F/190C/Gas 5. Brown the veal in the butter and add garlic and grated onion. Place in a covered casserole and then, in a pan, fry the sliced mushrooms and add to the meat. Add the beef bouillon, nutmeg, bay leaf and sliced waterchestnuts, salt and pepper. Stir and cover. Cook until tender in the oven, about 1-1½ hours. Remove bay leaf and add cream. Cook uncovered for a further 15 minutes and sprinkle with parsley just before serving.

Escalope of Veal Elizabeth Mary   serves 1

This is named after the two great liners that preceded the QE2; the *Queen Mary* and the *Queen Elizabeth*. The QE2 has links with both; her international call sign is that of the Mary and the warning bell sounded when at anchor in fog is a recording of that used on the *Queen Elizabeth*.

Opposite:
The intimate Princess Grill.

1 small clove of garlic
1½ oz/37 g chopped onion
butter to cook
salt, pepper
1 veal escalope
¼ cup/2 oz/50 ml sweet sherry
⅛ cup/1 fl oz/25 ml Bacardi rum
2½ fl oz/75 ml cream
asparagus tips to garnish

Rub a frying pan with the garlic, add butter and melt and then add onion. Season to taste and cook until brown. Place well flattened veal escalope in the pan and pour over the sweet sherry. Cook until the liqueur has been reduced. Flame the meat with the rum. Extinguish the flame with the cream and serve garnished with asparagus tips.

Veal Scaloppine with Marsala serves 4

1½ lb/675 g boneless veal steak
flour to coat
salt, freshly ground black pepper
2 tbs/30 ml vegetable oil
1 tb/15 ml butter
8 oz/225 g thinly sliced mushrooms
1 finely minced clove of garlic
2 tbs/30 ml finely chopped parsley
1 tsp/5 ml dried basil
1 cup/8 oz/225 g peeled, de-seeded and
    chopped tomatoes
½ cup plus 2 tbs/¼ pint/150 ml
    Marsala wine

Preheat the oven to 350F/180C/Gas 4. Pound the veal with a meat mallet until thin. Cut into 2 in/5 cm squares and coat the pieces with flour. Sprinkle meat with salt and pepper. Heat the oil and butter in a frying pan and brown the meat on all sides. Transfer meat to a casserole. Add the mushrooms and garlic to the frying pan and cook briefly. Add the remaining ingredients to the pan and pour the mixture over the veal in the casserole. Cover and bake in the oven for about 45 minutes.

Veal kidneys are cooked tableside and flamed with brandy for this dinner dish.

Veal Kidneys Flambé serves 4

2 tbs/30 ml oil
½ cup/4 oz/125 g butter
8 kidneys (veal or lamb's can be used)
salt, freshly ground black pepper
4 chopped shallots
½ cup/4 oz/125 g mushrooms
4 measures brandy or armagnac
1¼ cup/½ pint/275 ml cream

Melt the oil and the butter in a pan and add the kidneys seasoned to taste. Add the chopped shallots, mushrooms (finely sliced) and brandy or armagnac. Flame the brandy and add cream, blend well, check seasoning and serve. The top of the dish can be finished off with truffle decoration and it should be served with rice pilaff, buttered noodles, or riced potatoes and green vegetables, or a salad.

Beef, of course, remains number one meat favourite, especially with American passengers, although the British tend to opt more for fish dishes. The 150,000 best beef fillets picked up in New York for a World Cruise can be served 1 lb in weight and 3 inches thick if wished. In the dining room they can be flamed as **Steak Diane** or served **Tartare** style for dieters. For special evenings, **Fillet Etna** is served cooked in butter in a pan and covered with a slice of Mozzarella cheese and asparagus tips; simple but very tasty. Another dinner dish is **Beef President** with a mushroom and sherry sauce.

Beef President
serves 2

2 tbs/30 ml butter
2 x 12 oz/350 g thin slices of beef fillet
6 sliced, cooked carrots
6 cooked potatoes

Melt the butter in a pan and cook meat on both sides until cooked as required. Add the cooked vegetables, the potatoes diced finely and cover with **President Sauce** (see below)

President Sauce

2 tbs/30 ml butter
1 cup/8 oz/225 g sliced mushrooms
2 tbs/30 ml sherry
1 tsp/5 ml cornstarch (cornflour)
1¼ cups/½ pint/275 ml beef consommé
1 oz/25 g tomato purée
salt, pepper

Heat a pan and add butter and mushrooms. Cook until tender. Stir in sherry thickened with cornstarch dissolved in a little water. Add beef consommé and tomato purée, season to taste and simmer until well blended. Spoon over meat and vegetables.

Beef Medallions and Rice
serves 4

4 fillet minute steaks
salt, freshly ground black pepper
2 tbs/30 ml butter   *(continued)*

Season steaks with salt and pepper. Melt half the butter in a frying pan and quickly stir in sage, basil and mustard. Add steaks and cook as required. Place

¼ tsp/1.2 ml ground sage
¼ tsp/1.2 ml basil
1 tsp/5 ml Dijon mustard
¾ cup/6 oz/175 g cooked, white or wild rice
2 tsps/10 ml capers
1 glass dry white wine

steaks on a base of cooked rice and keep hot. Add the remaining butter, capers and white wine to the frying pan and boil rapidly with meat juices, then pour over the steaks.

A warming country style casserole is named after a part of Australia, which the ship visits on her Pacific Cruises.

Queensland Beef Casserole *serves 4*

4 cups/2 lb/1 kg ground (minced) sirloin beef
2 large onions
2 green peppers
1 stalk celery
salt, pepper
1¼ cups/½ pint/275 ml tomato soup
1¼ cups/½ pint/275 ml mushroom soup
8 oz/225 g noodles
1 lb/450 g sliced cheddar cheese
10 oz/275 g button mushrooms
½ tsp/2.5 ml dried herbs

Simmer the meat in a large pan and add chopped onions, peppers, celery and soups and cook until tender. Cook noodles in salted boiling water, rinse and drain. Mix with the meat and vegetables in a large casserole. Place the sliced cheese on top of the meat and arrange button mushrooms and herbs in the mixture. Cook in the oven at 300F/150C/Gas 2 for 45 minutes or until the cheese melts and the casserole bubbles.

Simple dishes are much liked by many of the passengers. Joe Loss, who at 21, was Britain's youngest bandleader in 1930, is a favourite with the British Royal Family who ask his band to play for their private parties. Joe, who provides the music for nightly dancing in the Double Down Room — the largest entertainment room afloat — on all the QE2's major cruises, flew home from one to play for Her Majesty the Queen at Windsor Castle for her fiftieth birthday. Joe Loss enjoys stews and casseroles on board and one of his favourite dishes is a simple cottage pie, called **Farmhouse Pie.**

Farmhouse Pie *serves 4*

1 oz/25 g butter
4 oz/125 g diced carrots
1 cup/8 oz/225 g chopped onions
2 cups/1 lb/450 g ground (minced) beef
1 tb/15 ml tomato purée
1 tsp/5 ml mixed herbs
salt, pepper
1 ¼ cups/½ pint/275 ml beef stock
1 tsp/5 ml cornstarch (cornflour)
for potato topping:
1 lb/450 g potatoes
1 tb/15 ml cream
milk to mix
salt, pepper
2 egg yolks

Melt butter in a large heavy pan and cook vegetables in this until softened but not browned. Add beef and cook well, stirring frequently. Add tomato purée and herbs, salt and pepper. Cook well through with the beef stock, thickened slightly with the cornstarch dissolved in a little water. Place meat mixture in an ovenproof dish and cook for 30 minutes in a moderate oven (350F/180C/Gas 4). Make mashed potato topping by cooking peeled potatoes until soft. Drain off cooking water and beat with a large fork with milk, cream and seasoning, until fluffy. Then beat in the two egg yolks which will give a good glazed finish. Cover the top of the meat with the potatoes and decorate with the back of a fork making the potato smooth. Replace in the oven until heated through or until needed.

Another very low cost, humble recipe is **Scouse**, a beef stew originating in Liverpool, the former home of Cunard company and still home to many of the crew on the QE2 who are nicknamed Scouse after their home town.

Scouse *serves 8*

2 lb/1 kg any inexpensive cut of beef,
    such as shin
3 onions
2 leeks
1 small swede (yellow turnip)
3 carrots
1 head of celery
salt, pepper
4 potatoes

Dice the meat and vegetables and place all together in a large pan. Cover with water and add salt and pepper to taste. Allow to cook over a low heat for about 3½ hours. Add diced potatoes one hour before serving.

Though the restaurant's Head Waiters are always interested to hear of a new recipe from passengers, they occasionally get together and think up new ideas themselves which they try out at their own lunches, after service. **Lamb Cutlets Orientale** is one such idea in which cutlets are fried gently in a pan with a few spoonfuls of honey and soya sauce and seasoning to taste. Restaurant Manager of the Queen's Grill, Ron Pitcher, says that when cooking meat in a frying pan, it is always a flavour tip to de-glaze (swill it out) with a drop of sherry or even cider and add this to the gravy or sauce to give the meat extra taste.

The following idea originated at London's Reform Club in the last century and is an attractive way of glamorising lamb cutlets for a dinner party. On the QE2 a piquant redcurrant flavour is added to the sauce. Prepare 2 or 3 lamb cutlets for each person by beating with a meat mallet. Dip in beaten egg mixed with a dash of milk and then coat in white breadcrumbs mixed with finely minced ham and finely chopped parsley. Cook the cutlets slowly in butter in a heavy pan and serve coated with the **Reform Sauce** (see below).

Reform Sauce   *for 4–6 servings*

2½ cups/1 pint/450 ml brown sauce (made by cooking pieces of vegetables in meat juices until brown, with herbs, seasoning and tomato trimmings and thickened with 1 tsp/5ml cornstarch (cornflour) dissolved in a little water).
6 oz/175 g redcurrant jelly
1 oz/25 ml sherry
fine strips of beetroot, white of hard-boiled eggs, small sliced gherkins and strips of ox tongue to garnish

Add the redcurrant jelly to the brown sauce and simmer with the sherry until melted and hot, Finally, before serving add in strips of beetroot, hard-boiled egg white, small gherkins and ox tongue and heat through before serving over the lamb cutlets.

Roast Loin of Pork appears on many of the QE2 menus and is well liked. To cut the fattiness of pork, Chef John Bainbridge makes **Gooseberry and Ginger Sauce** when he has fruit left over.

Gooseberry and Ginger Sauce

serves 4

4 oz/125 g gooseberries
1½ tbs/22 ml sugar
ginger to taste
4 oz/125 g redcurrant jelly
1 tsp/5ml cornstarch (cornflour)

Simmer the gooseberries with the sugar and ginger to taste, until soft. Add the redcurrant jelly and thicken sauce with the cornstarch dissolved in a little water. Serve with roast dishes instead of apple sauce.

Ham, too, makes an elegant dinner dish cut into small baton pieces QE2 style and flamed in brandy with a wine sauce.

Batons of Ham Flambé

serves 4

⅛ cup/1 oz/25 g butter
⅛ cup/1 oz/25 g sugar
1 tsp/5 ml vinegar
1 glass red wine
1 oz/25 g redcurrant jelly
1 wine glass tomato ketchup
½ tsp/2.5 ml Worcester sauce
½ tsp/2.5 ml cornstarch (cornflour)
chopped gherkins to taste
1½ lb/675 g boiled gammon, cut into
   batons or finger shaped pieces
1 glass brandy
½ cup plus 2 tbs/¼ pint/150 ml cream
salt, freshly ground black pepper
paprika

Melt the butter in a frying pan and add the sugar, vinegar and cook until browned and caramelised. Gradually add the wine and redcurrant jelly. Add the tomato ketchup, Worcester sauce and cornstarch dissolved in a little water. Simmer and stir well until thickened. Add gherkins and the ham and mix thoroughly with the sauce. Add brandy and flame (Benedictine can be used as an alternative liqueur). Extinguish the flame by adding the cream; add seasoning and dust the top of the dish with a little paprika. Serve with buttered noodles and haricots verts.

Chicken is a good light meat and can be simply cooked as **Chicken in the Pot,** a recipe which also appears on the ship's Kosher menu and is liked by Ann Brooks from Los Angeles, a passenger who has taken all of the ship's nine World Cruises to date. Ann sits at the Captain's Table in the Columbia Restaurant and pre-orders this dish.

Chicken in the Pot
serves 4

3–4 lb/1½–2 kg chicken
chicken stock to cover
2 onions
1 bay leaf
bouquet garni
3 oz/75 g narrow noodles
salt, freshly ground black pepper

Boil the chicken gently in the stock with the chopped onions, bay leaf, bouquet garni and seasoning to taste for about 45 minutes. Remove the chicken, skin and cut into portion-sized pieces (alternatively the chicken can be left whole and carved at table). Cook noodles in the boiling chicken stock and replace the chicken pieces in the pot. Remove the bay leaf and bouquet garni and adjust seasoning.

Chicken Florentine
serves 6

2 cups/1 lb/450 g cooked, chopped
    spinach
1 crushed clove of garlic
½ oz/12 g marjoram
½ oz/12 g oregano
1 tb/15 ml flour
3 oz/75 ml cream
the meat from 1 roasted chicken (about 5
    lb/2½ kg size)
3 tbs/45 ml butter
3 tbs/45 ml flour
¾ cup/6 fl oz/175 ml cream
¾ cup/6 fl oz/175 ml chicken stock
salt, pepper
1 cup/9 oz/250 g Parmesan cheese

Mix garlic, flour and cream to the well drained, cooked spinach. Spread the mixture over the bottom of an ovenproof dish and cover with chopped or shredded chicken meat. Melt the butter and stir in the flour, add stock and cream and stir well and heat until the sauce becomes thick. Season to taste. Pour sauce over the chicken and cover with the cheese. Bake in a moderate oven at 350F/180C/Gas 4 for about 2 minutes until the cheese is bubbling.

Opposite:
Flambé meat in the Queen's Grill.

Turkey appears on the menu at times other than Christmas, July 4th and Thanksgiving Day, with 5,000 lb put aboard for every transatlantic crossing. This rolled breast of turkey recipe was created by Chef Bainbridge for one of the Purser's staff.

Turkey Francemil

serves 4

4 slices of turkey breast each ½ in/1 cm
    thick
salt, freshly ground black pepper
4 slices prosciutto
1 cup/8 oz/225 g cooked spinach
pinch nutmeg
flour for coating
butter for cooking
for Rich Red Wine Sauce:
butter for cooking
¼ cup/2 oz/50 g minced shallots
1 clove of garlic, minced
1 cup/8 oz/225 g sliced mushrooms
2½ cups/1 pint/575 ml red burgundy
    wine
1¼ cups/½ pint/275 ml chicken stock
1 tsp/5 ml cornstarch (cornflour)
1 tsp/5 ml freshly chopped parsley

Flatten the turkey slices with a meat mallet. Season to taste with salt and pepper. Place a slice of prosciutto on each slice of turkey. Finely chop the drained spinach seasoned with salt, pepper and nutmeg and place on top of the prosciutto. Fold in the sides of the turkey meat and shape into a roll about 2 in/5 cm long. Secure with a cocktail stick. Lightly dust with flour and brown in butter. Remove cocktail stick and place rolls in a casserole and cover with the Rich Red Wine Sauce made by browning the finely minced shallots with the garlic and mushrooms. Add wine and chicken stock and simmer for 30 minutes to reduce amount of liquid. Thicken slightly with the cornstarch dissolved in a little water. Bake in the oven for 30 minutes at 350F/180C/Gas 4.

4 THE CAPTAIN'S TABLE
Special Recipes for Special Evenings

There is something about the sea that seems to make people want to celebrate and the myth that captains can marry couples on board died hard. Edwina Sandys, Churchill's grand-daughter, did try to be married on the QE2 but the Captain, first checking with a call to his vicar at home, found he had no way of performing that ceremony. The QE2 did, however, have a wedding buffet on board in New York harbour before she sailed on her 1983 Pacific Cruise. Birthdays and anniversaries are marked by waiters bringing on to complete the dinner, a special birthday cake — complete with one tactful candle — made from a light sponge mix and carefully iced.

Though dress codes are not as strict as once they were, the ship's daily programme suggests formal or informal or optional dressing for the evening. On one World Cruise, one lady took an adjacent cabin just for her clothes and wore a different outfit every evening for the 90 days. Another lady would wear two different evening gowns each night. Even the restaurants make an effort to dress for dinner with the

Columbia changing its table linen from creams and lemons of the day to face-flattering pink.

The Captain's cocktail party night, when everyone is invited to champagne and canapés, is held in the public rooms; the light gold and cream Queen's Room or dramatic Double Down Room of seductive scarlet tweeds and plum suede snuggeries with glittering silver chrome highlights and a 24-feet wide spiral staircase. This night is always formal and passengers tend to order a special dinner for the occasion. The waiters have lists of special dishes with which to tempt passengers into choosing something glamorous. In the Queen's Grill these include some light and nouvelle cuisine inspired ideas and some ideas contributed by Michael Quinn of the Ritz Hotel in London (see Chapter 10).

The favourite special orders throughout the ship are **Beef Wellington, Rack of Lamb, Chateaubriand,** (rare for Americans, well done for Britons), **Steaks Diane** or **Tartare** (to which Ron Pitcher in the Queen's Grill adds a touch of brandy), **Lobster Thermidor, Veal Piccata, Duckling à l'Orange** (flamed in orange curacao) or **Duckling Montmorency** (flamed in kirsch).

There are in fact *two* Captain's Tables on the QE2 and the Captain and the Staff Captain alternate between them so passengers in both the Columbia and the Tables of the World Restaurants get a glimpse of the Master. In the Columbia his table is set just beyond the buffet on which stands a 30 inch high solid silver, elaborately moulded, pot, the only thing on the ship seen and touched by Samuel Cunard, the founder of the line. The silver pot, which has lost its lid, and which itself went missing for fifty years, was presented to Samuel Cunard by the citizens of Boston to mark the start of a transatlantic sea service to that city in 1840. In the Tables of the World, the Captain sits in the central oriental section under wall lights made of oriental fans and near an impressive indoor pagoda, reflected in a mirror, with silvered walls and a gold leaf ceiling.

Captain's Table favourites according to Joan

Arnott, wife of Captain Bob, the current master, are crêpes, **Saddle of Lamb, Steak Diane,** followed by **Soufflé Nassau,** in which oranges are scooped out and filled with a vanilla and orange soufflé mixture and cooked so the soufflé mushrooms up from the fruit shell which is served set on a slice of pineapple. The Arnotts' own favourite, a nouvelle cuisine style recipe from the Queen's Grill's list of special orders is duck with green peppercorns now named after them.

Duck Arnott
serves 5

2 well cooked ducks
1 cup/8 fl oz/225 ml cream
3 oz/75 g green peppercorns
a little brandy
salt
4 medium cooking apples
demarara sugar to cook

Remove skin and meat from the bone of the roasted ducks and slice the breast and other meat very finely. Swirl cream in a heavy frying pan and simmer the green peppercorns in it until reduced and thickened. Add a little brandy and seasoning to taste. Place duck slices on a serving dish and cover with the sauce and keep hot. Meanwhile blanch peeled, cored apples by

Duck Arnott at the Captain's Table.

plunging into boiling water for a few minutes. In a heatproof dish, cover apple slices with demarara sugar and place under the grill until the sugar caramelises. Serve around the duck.

Although the staunch favourite main dish remains beef, it is dressed up for special evenings. Tournedos may be served Marguéry style, fried in butter on croûtons of fried bread with a sauce made in the pan at the table. Port wine is swilled round, reduced with heavy (double) cream as required, seasoned, and poured over the Tournedos which is served with quartered lamb's kidneys and mushrooms and perhaps a few blanched, whole, cooked tomatoes.

Steak au Poivre à la Crème *serves 4*

4 boneless sirloin steaks about ¾ lb/350
    g each
2 tbs/50 g or more, black peppercorns
salt
vegetable oil
2½ oz/62 g butter
2 tbs/50 g finely chopped shallots or
    green onions
3 fl oz/75 ml warmed cognac
2½ cups/1 pint/575 ml heavy (double)
    cream
1 tb/15 ml Dijon or Dusseldorf mustard

Trim off most of the fat on the steaks. Using a pestle and mortar or the bottom of a heavy pan, pound the peppercorns until roughly crushed. Pour crushed pepper onto a piece of waxed paper and dredge the steaks with the pepper on both sides. Press the pepper into the steaks with the palm of the hand. Sprinkle lightly on both sides with salt. Place a heavy pan on the stove and brush lightly with oil. When oil is hot, add the steaks and cook over a medium heat until brown on both sides; about 7 minutes each side. Cook further until cooked to taste. Remove steaks and keep hot, pouring off any surplus fat. Cover steaks with foil and keep hot. Wipe out the pan with paper towels and add butter and shallots. Cook, stirring, for about 3 minutes but do not brown the onions. Add brandy and light it; add the cream and cook, stirring frequently, for about 10 minutes. Remove pan from the heat and stir in mustard, do not cook further. Pour hot sauce over steaks and serve at once.

Though the Queen's Grill has been asked to serve a Stiltonburger for a touch of class, it is chicken that gets the big cheese treatment in this rich recipe devised by Chef Derrick Leigh for guests in the Grill.

Chicken Stilton

serves 4

4 skinned breasts of chicken
4 oz/125 g Stilton cheese
2 oz/50 g finely chopped celery
2 oz/50 g finely chopped walnuts
½ cup/4 oz/125 g wild rice
½ cup plus 2 tbs/¼ pint/150 ml white wine
salt, freshly ground black pepper
flour to coat
butter to cook
½ cup plus 2 tbs/¼ pint/150 ml red wine
½ cup plus 2 tbs/¼ pint/150 ml port wine
2 tbs/30 ml redcurrant jelly
2½ cups/1 pint/575 ml heavy (double) cream
½ cup/2 oz/50 g flaked almonds

Flatten each chicken breast as thin as possible with a meat mallet. Mix together the Stilton, celery, and walnuts to make a paste. Form into four, finger shaped pieces. Place one on each chicken breast (as for **Chicken Kiev**) and roll chicken meat round securing with a cocktail stick. Place in the fridge to set. Cook wild rice in water with white wine and seasoning to taste. When cooked, leave in the pan to cool and drain when cool. Coat chicken pieces with flour, carefully remove the cocktail sticks and cook until sealed in a hot pan with a little butter. Remove chicken and keep hot. Add red wine, port wine and redcurrant jelly to the pan. When the jelly has dissolved, add the cream and almonds and simmer until the sauce thickens. Pour over the chicken then cover chicken with foil and cook in the oven at 300F/150C/Gas 2 for 20 minutes. Serve surrounded by hot wild rice with the sauce poured over the chicken.

Chef John Bainbridge introduced venison, hare and frog's legs to the ship for the 1977 Jubilee World Cruise and many types of game including grouse and quail are carried. This venison recipe is a ship's speciality named after the QE2's Austrian chef, Karl Winkler.

Venison Winkler

serves 6

6 x 8 oz/225 g venison steaks
¾ cup/6 oz/175 g fat for larding   *(cont)*

Thread venison steaks with fat to lard them and marinate for 36 hours in the oil, red wine, bay leaves,

for marinade:
2½ cups/1 pint/575 ml red wine
thinly sliced carrots, turnips, celery,
*   onions*
2 bay leaves
salt, pepper
nutmeg
1 oz/25 g juniper berries
½ cup/4 fl oz/125 ml vegetable oil
1 tb/15 ml flour
½ cup/4 fl oz/125 ml sour cream
6 fresh pears
¼ cup/2 oz/50 g sugar
1 cup/6 oz/225 g cranberries

juniper berries, thinly sliced vegetables and seasonings. Remove steaks from marinade and quickly seal in a hot frying pan using oil from the marinade. Thicken juices with flour and add the thinly sliced vegetables, bring to the boil and simmer for 30 minutes in marinade mixture. Add the sour cream, remove steaks and strain the sauce over them. Serve with potato croquettes and the pears poached until tender in sugar and water with the cranberries.

Brandied Terrine of Duck *serves about 10*

1 duck
12 oz/350 g pork
12 oz/350 g chicken
3 eggs
½ cup plus 2 tbs/¼ pint/150 ml brandy
½ tsp/2.5 ml mixed spices
salt, freshly ground black pepper
for garnish:
sweet gherkins, pistacchio nuts, tinned
*   ox tongue, liverwurst, stuffed olives*

Remove skin from cooked duck keeping skin whole if possible. Remove meat from the carcase. Put skin on one side. Place duck meat and all the other ingredients except the garnishings, into a chopping machine and blend to a smooth paste. Line a terrine dish or baking mould with greased cooking foil and line again with the duck skin. Place a third of the mixture over the bottom of the mould and add on top, decorative strips of tinned ox tongue, liverwurt, stuffed sliced olives, sweet sliced gherkins or pistacchio nuts to taste. Cover with a second layer of the mixture and gently press down. Add more decorative strips and cover with the remaining third of the mixture bringing the duck skins over and sealing with greased foil. Place in a baking dish containing water to come about half way up the sides of the terrine and cook at 375F/190C/Gas 5 for 2 hours. Allow to cool and remove from the mould.

Opposite:
Beef Wellington – one of the ship's
most popular specialities.

There are always plenty of occasions for a celebration menu; annual dates like Christmas, Easter, St Patrick's and Burn's Nights, the last complete with haggis and tatties and neeps, **Scottish Mixed Grill** and **Scottish Raspberry Soufflé.** July 4th features chilled, brandied **Maine Lobster Bisque,** creamed Alaskan king crabmeat rolled in fillets of sole and coated with lobster sauce and roast Vermont turkey with savoury chestnut and sausage stuffing and cranberry sauce which is also served for Thanksgiving.

Christmas is a very special occasion at sea. In 1982 special preview lunches were given on board in Southampton to give people the chance to enjoy a Christmas meal on board. A champagne reception preceded the five course menu which started with **Shrimp Cocktail** and finished with **Grand Marnier Soufflé.** At sea, there are specially decorated buffets, Christmas trees, champagne parties and the traditional fare no matter how hot the outside temperature — the ship is usually in the Caribbean for Christmas.

Preparation starts early in the season. I have watched the cooks make 1,700 individual Christmas puddings while bouncing though the fringe of a hurricane in November. The mix for the ship's Christmas pudding 'for 2,500 souls' as the recipe is headed, is astounding in amount. The mix includes 90 lb of currants, 60 lb sultanas, 60 lb raisins, 30 lb mixed peel, 60 lb chopped suet, 24 lb apples, 48 lb breadcrumbs, 48 lb sugar, 48 lb flour, 7½ lb ground almonds, 240 eggs, the juices of 80 oranges and lemons, 4 lb mixed spices, and 2 bottles of rum and 2 of brandy. The Christmas cake, complete with marzipan and icing covering is no less lavish with 80 lb currants, 60 lb butter, 60 lb sugar, 3 bottles of sherry and 65 lb flour among its ingredients.

The ship also had to think on a mammoth scale when she was commissioned by the British Government to carry troops to the Falklands in 1982. Already stocked for a cruise, the ship added in more stores to cope with a possible six months trip and set off packed with 3,500 soldiers and 700 crew. The troops were delighted at the superb quality of food provided and the regimental cooks helped in the ship's galley in battle dress, complete with guns. The soldiers enjoyed a nightcap of the ship's baker's sticky Chelsea buns and tea while the officers, 360 of them dined in two sittings in the Queen's Grill. The Gurkha regiments on board ate the same lunch as the rest but in the evening their own cooks went to the galley to make their traditional curries.

On the return trip the ship realised that in spite of giving food to the mine sweepers she still had plenty of stores left while fresh food was scarce, the ship's chefs thought up this store cupboard pudding which could help a housewife through winter if she needs a cheap, nourishing family pudding.

Macaroni Pudding   *serves 4*

2½ cups/1 pint/575 ml milk
2½ oz/75 g/30 ml elbow macaroni
1 tb/15 ml sugar
pinch nutmeg
pinch salt
1 tsp/5 ml cornstarch (cornflour)

Boil the macaroni in the milk with the sugar, nutmeg and salt until macaroni is tender. Slightly thicken with the cornstarch dissolved in a little water. Pour into a pie dish and bake in a moderate oven (350F/180C/Gas 4) for about 30 minutes.

More joyous occasions are those associated with the Royal Family. The ship was honoured in December 1982 when Her Majesty Queen Elizabeth the Queen Mother came to lunch and to unveil a plaque in honour of those who had travelled to South Georgia in the QE2. The brigade heads of the regiments carried, and Cunard's directors were present at Southampton docks for the occasion. The plaque is now situated between the Royal Standards on the stairway outside the casino.

At the special lunch in the Queen's Grill, the Queen Mother was seated at an extra large table which could seat twelve people. The table, specially made for the occasion, is now referred to as the

'Queen Mother's Tabletop' and is used when passengers request extra large seating groups in the Columbia Restaurant.

The menu designed for the Queen Mother bore in mind that Her Majesty was still recovering from a throat operation a week earlier. It was prepared by Chef John Bainbridge and began with a coquille dish, continued with **Roast Rack of Southdown Lamb** and ended with fresh pears cooked in Grand Marnier.

Coquille Royale
serves 4

16 slices lobster meat
1¼ cups/½ pint/275 ml fish stock (made by boiling fish scraps with onions and herbs and reducing liquid well)
2 cups minus 1 tb/¾ pint/425 ml heavy (double) cream
½ cup plus 2 tbs/¼ pint/150 ml white wine
2 egg yolks
salt, freshly ground black pepper
4 oz/125 g sliced cooked mushrooms
2 oz/50 g cooked minced shallots
cooked strips of leek and celery to garnish

Place 4 slices of lobster per serving, in a heatproof china scallop shell or individual gratin dish. In a pan mix fish stock with the cream and white wine. Stir well and thicken by adding the egg yolks, taking care not to let the mixture boil. Season to taste and mix in mushrooms and shallots and cover the lobster with the sauce. Decorate the top with leek and celery strips cooked in butter. Glaze under the grill until just browned.

Whole Pears Poached in Liqueur
serves 4

4 whole ripe pears
1 cup/8 oz/225 g sugar
2½ cups/1 pint/575 ml water
lemon juice
½ cup/4 oz/125 ml Grand Marnier
grated orange peel
1 tsp/5 ml cornstarch (cornflour) or arrowroot

Peel the pears, but leave a little of the stem on top. Slice a small piece off the bottom so the pears stand firmly on the dish and scoop out the core with an apple corer. Poach the pears gently in a syrup made by cooking together the sugar, water and lemon juice. When the pears are tender, remove from the syrup. Boil the syrup further to reduce it and add the Grand Marnier and finely grated orange peel. Thicken with the cornstarch or arrowroot dissolved in a little water. Pour over the pears in individual serving dishes. Serve with whipped cream.

One of the most memorable meals on board was the gala dinner created by Chef Bainbridge to celebrate the wedding of Prince Charles and Lady Diana on July 29th, 1981. The QE2 was nearing England on a transatlantic crossing but video tapes of the wedding were flown to the ship by helicopter and a special champagne reception was given by the Captain with a gala dinner and ball afterwards.

The dark blue and gold menu cards tied with a scarlet cord carried profiles of the royal couple and the crest of the Prince of Wales and are now collectors' items. The dishes, after an opening Beluga caviare serving, were named after people and places associated with the couple. Between the entrée and dessert was an avocado pear with grapefruit and walnuts throat-soother with a Spencer dressing. Among the desserts was **Soufflé Bowes Lyon,** named after the Queen Mother; a festive two-tone vanilla and chocolate soufflé with a hot chocolate sauce.

Soufflé Bowes Lyon   *serves 4*

½ cup/4 oz/125 g butter
1 cup/4 oz/125 g flour
1¼ cups/½ pint/275 ml milk
⅛ cup/1 oz/25g cocoa powder
a few drops vanilla essence
8 eggs, separated
¼ cup/2 oz/ 50 g sugar
butter and sugar for moulds

Mix butter and flour together and bring the milk to the boil. Add the flour mixture and stir well and cook until sauce has thickened. Divide mixture into half and add cocoa powder to one half and vanilla essence to the other. Add 4 egg yolks to each half mixture and mix until smooth. Beat sugar with the egg whites to a stiff firm foam and fold equal amounts into each half mixture. Butter and sugar the inside of a large soufflé dish and carefully place the two halves on top of each other in the dish. Place soufflé dish in a pan containing hot water about half way up the sides and cook at 350F/180C/Gas 4 for 35 minutes. Serve with a hot chocolate sauce (see page 85).

It is with the dessert course on the QE2 that much of the glamour of a meal comes, especially with the flambé work carried out by the Head Waiters and Restaurant Managers in the four restaurants. Roy Hayhurst, Restaurant Manager of the Columbia Restaurant, joined Cunard in 1949 and served on the *Britannia,* the *Carinthia,* the *Media* and the *Queen Mary* before coming to the QE2. He says flambé work is a novelty to many and is now found, correctly done, in fewer and fewer restaurants ashore. On a World Cruise, he and his five Head Waiters create **Crêpes Suzette, Cherries Jubilee** and **Baked Alaska,** which he says are the three most popular special desserts on the ship — though **Banana Foster** is fast catching up.

The standard crêpes batter, used for many recipes both savoury and sweet, is made as follows.

Crêpes Batter

makes about 10–12 pancakes 5 ins/12½ cm in diameter

¾ cup/6 oz/175 g sifted flour
2 tsp/10 ml sugar
½ tsp/2.5 ml salt
¾ cup/6 fl oz/175 ml milk
3 lightly beaten eggs

Mix flour, sugar and salt. Add milk alternatively with the eggs. Beat until smooth. Grease the bottom of a heavy, small frying pan. When very hot, cover the bottom of the pan with a thin layer of batter and tilt until the crêpe is paper thin and even. Brown gently on both sides and keep crêpes until needed in greaseproof paper sheets. The crêpes can be made ahead of time and reheated as required in the oven.

David Chambers, Restaurant Manager of the Princess Grill, who comes from the Isle of Wight and who joined the QE2 four weeks before her launch in Scotland, says **Crêpes QE2,** using the above crêpes, is a popular dish. The thin crêpes are rolled round cigar-shaped pieces of vanilla ice-cream and deep frozen. The Head Waiters make the traditional **Crêpes Suzette** sauce with sugar 2 oz/50 g butter and juice of half a lemon and half an orange, in their pans

MENU

Beluga Malossol Caviar, Royale
(Special Reserve for this Occasion)

Cocktail of Crabmeat Claw, Duchy of Cornwall

******

Clear Turtle Consomme, Prince of Wales
(Polo Batons)

Potage, Caernarvon Castle

******

Delice of Dover Sole, Bronington

Crayfish Tails from the Scottish Isles, Balmoral

******

Broiled Prime Tenderloin Steak, Lady Diana

Roast Rack of Spring Lamb from the Cotswolds, Prince Charles

Asparagus Spears, Badminton   Whole Green Beans, St. Pauls

Elizabeth Potatoes

******

Avocado Pear with Grapefruit Segments and Walnuts, Highgrove House

Spencer Dressing

******

Souffle, Bowes-Lyon

Coupe, Althorp House

Sandringham Delights

Sherbet, Gordonstoun

******

Commonwealth Coffee   Galaxy of Summer Fruits

A special occasion:
The Royal Wedding, 29 July 1981

by the tables and quickly place the frozen crêpes in the pan to thaw them out and cook, but not quite melt, the ice-cream. The crêpes are then flamed in brandy or orange curacao and topped with a scattering of almond macaroons and finely grated chocolate. A tip from the Queen's Grill for cooking crêpes is to place a piece of orange peel in the pan. The oil from it moves the sugar and prevents it sticking, and also stops the fork from scratching the pan.

The first flame to flare on each voyage, soon spurs a flood of requests for blazing liqueur desserts and the restaurants flicker with the lights of flash cameras and heating lamps. **Bombe Vesuvius** is an old but dramatic Cunard favourite. A Baked Alaska sponge, topped with ice-cream and meringue mixture, is made up in the shape of a volcano and cooked quickly. A halved egg shell of brandy is set in the top of the 'volcano' which has its sides streaked with 'lava' made from cochineal coloured jelly or melted redcurrant jelly and the whole is served with the brandy flaming and smoking from the 'crater'. Raspberries flamed in kirsch can be served with this dish.

David Calder treats that rather awkward fruit, the kiwi, to the flambé finish by peeling, slicing into a pan with melted sugar and flaming in kirsch. Slices of pineapple on the QE2 are cooked in butter and sugar on a chafing dish and flamed in brandy and served coated with melted blackcurrant jam.

Ron Pitcher has served thirty years with Cunard and went to the QE2 from the *Queen Elizabeth* to open the Princess Grill. He now works in the Queen's Grill where he often serves **Flamed Triple Fruits.** Any three fruits suitably contrasting in colour can be used. Ron Pitcher divides his flambé pan into triangles of black cherries, white grapes and mandarin oranges, cooks them in 2–3 tbs/30–45 ml clear honey and then flames them in lots of kirsch.

Another of his inventions is **Crêpes Mary Louise.** In an omelette pan, heat a small can of mandarin oranges and clear honey — about 2–3 tbs/30–45 ml enough to cover the pan bottom. When the honey is hot and bubbling, scatter ginger to taste until the mixture is thick and creamy in appearance. Mix with a fork and add in two thin crêpes (see page 67) and fold around the oranges. Flame the dish with generous measure of orange curacao.

Another Queen's Grill speciality from Mr Pitcher, who recently reintroduced the elegant habit of having the Restaurant Managers of the two grill rooms wear full, tailed, evening suits for formal nights on board, is **Bananas Caribbean.** This serves 2. Cover the bottom of an omelette pan with caster sugar and heat through until the sugar browns and caramelises. Place bananas (cut lengthways) cut side up in the pan, allowing one banana per person. Turn and sprinkle with flaked almonds. Flame the bananas with dark rum. On the QE2 this is served with a pistacchio bombe ice-cream. The almonds should be caramelised and crispy and the whole is served over the ice-cream not beside it.

There is a subtle art in getting liqueurs to flame well. The main secret is to heat the liqueurs very well before setting alight. On the ship, the Head Waiters use small poached-egg pans with the lids and poacher centres discarded and heat the generous shots of liqueur in these before lighting and pouring over the main pan and its contents. To make the flames go high and create a dramatic effect, heat one side of the main pan until extremely hot and smoking and pour the heated liqueur into this area. Waiters on the QE2 look carefully first to check that they are not working directly beneath one of the fire sprinklers before they go for a high flame of 3 or 4 feet.

A long established Cunard flamed dessert and a particular favourite of mine is **Cherries Jubilee.** Almost any fruit can be substituted for the big black Morello cherries used on board. To serve 2, melt 2 tbs/30 ml redcurrant jelly in a pan. Add 1½ tbs/22 ml white sugar scattered over the melted jelly and mix well. This will give a good glaze to the cherries. Stir in the cherries or other fruit and shake round the pan until well coated and hot. Finally flame the cherries in kirsch. I like these on their own but they can be served with a scoop of vanilla ice-cream. On board these cherries often accompany **Bombe Cyrano,** a cherry mousse mixture made with chopped crystallised cherries under a layer of praline, served on sponge cake, piped with whipped cream and decorated with cherries.

It is not surprising, with all this flame-throwing going on, that the ship's stocks of cooking wines are impressively big. The three most commonly used for flaming desserts are kirsch (250 bottles), curacao (350 bottles) and brandy (480 bottles) while 360 bottles of sherry and 36 bottles of maraschino make up the list — with 700 bottles of red and white wine for the galley to use. More flambé ideas using these liqueurs include **Bananas Flambé de luxe** and **Flambé Bananas Queen's Grill.**

Bananas Flambé de luxe *serves 3*

4 tbs/60 ml maple syrup
4 tbs/60 ml sugar
2 tbs/30 ml butter
juice of 2 limes
juice of 1 lemon
3 measures of dark rum
½ tsp/2.5 ml instant coffee
6 medium bananas

Heat a serving dish and frying pan. Add the maple syrup and butter to the pan. Allow to heat slightly and add the strained fruit juices stirring well. Add rum and coffee and finally the skinned bananas sliced lengthways. Cook quickly until lightly browned, turning occasionally, for 2–3 minutes. Spoon the sugar on top and pour the rum over the fruit; flame and serve.

Flambé Bananas Queen's Grill *serves 2*

2 firm, but ripe bananas
white sugar to cover pan base
1 orange
orange curacao/Grand Marnier to flame
dark rum to flame

Scatter the sugar evenly over the bottom of a wide omelette pan and heat through. Peel bananas and slice in half lengthways. Place cut side up on the sugar. Heat through until the sugar cararmelises and the banana tops are cooked; turn to the other side. Slice the orange in half and squeeze the juice out over the bananas with the aid of a fork. Heat a generous measure of orange curacao or Grand Marnier and flame bananas, then add another generous measure of dark rum and flame. In the Queen's Grill this dish is served spooned over an ice-cream bombe but is equally delicious on its own.

For the busy hostess, David Calder suggests slicing the bananas as above and placing on the sugar and orange juice in an ovenproof dish in a hot oven. The bananas can be left to caramelise and cook while the guests are eating their main course and can then be flamed with the rum just before bringing to the table.

Up-dated and simplified versions of two grand evening recipes from the old Cunard liners used still on the QE2 are **Floating Islands on a Raspberry Sea** and **Caramel Empress.**

Floating Islands on a Raspberry Sea *serves 4*

4 egg whites
½ cup/4 oz/125 g caster sugar
15 fl oz/¾ pint/425 ml milk
for custard base:
5 egg yolks
½ cup/4 oz/125 g caster sugar
pinch of salt
a few drops vanilla essence
1 lb/450 g sweetened raspberries

Make a meringue mixture with the egg whites and caster sugar and spoon tablespoonfuls into the milk and simmer in the milk until set. Lift out carefully with a slotted spoon and put to one side. Use the milk from the poaching to make the custard sauce. Beat the egg yolks with the caster sugar and a pinch of salt. In a double boiler heat the milk and gently beat in the egg mixture allowing it to thicken slowly; then add a dash of vanilla essence. Allow the thickened custard to cook and chill it. Spread over the base of a serving dish and place the poached meringue on top. Decorate the dish with spoonfuls of fresh or frozen raspberries sweetened to taste. Whipped cream can also be added for decoration.

Caramel Empress *serves 4*

for sauce:
1¼ cups/10 oz/275 g sugar
1 tb/15 ml water   *(continued)*

Make sauce by placing sugar and water in a heavy pan and stir slowly until the sugar mixture begins to go brown. Allow to caramelise fully and remove from

for crème caramel:
2½ cups/1 pint/575 ml milk
4 eggs
¼ cup/2 oz/50 g sugar
a few drops of vanilla essence
for meringue:
2 egg whites
⅛ cup/1 oz/25 g caster sugar

the heat. Add 2½ oz/62 ml hot water. Slowly stir this water in so the mixture does not spit. Brown the mixture further on the heat and reduce a little in amount. Place in the base of the crème caramel mould to a depth of about ⅛ in/¼ cm and leave to become hard. (Tubes of ready made caramel are also available to save time). Beat together the ingredients of the crème caramel and pour in the mould. Stand mould in a baking pan containing water and cook at 350F/180C/Gas 4 until set making sure the water does not boil. Allow to cool. Beat the meringue sugar and egg whites until stiff and pipe around the edge of a serving dish big enough to take the crème caramel. Brown the meringue under the grill. Gently unmould the crème caramel and decorate the platter with peach halves, pear halves and pineapple slices. Finish with scoops of vanilla ice-cream just before serving.

5 AROUND THE WORLD IN 80 MENUS
Recipes from Everywhere

The *Queen Elizabeth 2* was the first Cunard liner built to lead a Gemini life. In summer she would make transatlantic voyages and when the Atlantic was cold and grey in winter, would seek the sun around the world. When she was being designed, engineers visited the Panama Canal to measure it carefully to make sure she could slip through it. Even now there is only an eighteen inch clearance in the locks, and the roofs of the lock-control houses have to be hinged down as the 118 feet wide bridge passes through the 110 feet wide by 1,000 feet long, locks. The QE2, at 963 feet long, is the largest passenger ship to go through, paying a costly 90,000 dollars each way for the privilege.

The QE2 has been through the Panama Canal many times since her first World Cruise in 1975 and has also been through the Suez Canal. She was the first western liner allowed into a mainland Chinese port (Dairen in 1979). She has been to all the Continents and wherever she goes, arouses much local interest. Two million Japanese came to Yokohama to see her, 3,000 crowded the jetty in Tahiti and in Auckland they ran special 'view cruises' round the great ship. When she sails out of Port Everglades at dusk, the lights of the apartments in the tall harbour-side blocks, flash on and off in salute and cars hoot their horns in reply to the ship's whistle blasts.

In the old days of transatlantic crossings, the food was a mixture of American, British and Escoffier classical French. On the QE2 now, that file in Chef Bainbridge's office marked 'recipes from everywhere' and his collection of international cookbooks are used more and more, both to host receptions at maiden ports of call and to give the passengers a taste of the cuisine of the area in which they are sailing.

For the latter, the ship's chefs are assisted by guest chefs from top hotels like the Mandarin in Hong Kong and Las Brisas in Acapulco, who come aboard at various ports during the World Cruise to prepare special menus of their country. No expense is spared to make the recipes as authentic as possible. The right ingredients are ordered well ahead of time to the chefs' specifications. Passengers on tours of the kitchen may overhear Chef Bainbridge ordering by telephone, 'twelve gallons of pepperoni' or a complex list of Mexican spices for recipes like **Fish Balls Michilchiltextli** and **Pork Ribs in Achiote Sauce** — for which 200 oranges alone were used.

In addition to visiting chefs there are Austrian and Japanese chefs as well as a Kosher chef on the kitchen strength. Karl Winkler, from Salzburg, worked in golf and luncheon clubs in the States and at Cunard's Bristol Hotel in London before joining the QE2 for her first World Cruise. One of his native cuisine creations is a dessert from his own area; **Salzburger**

Opposite:
The Japanese chef puts the finishing touches to roast sucking pig.

Nockerln (see page 82), in which the meringue rises like the peaks of his home mountains.

Japanese meals can be ordered at any time for a lighter food, pleasing in presentation. These recipes are simplified ideas which can be copied at home.

Appetiser Omelettes

serves 4

These are small, square pieces of omelette with a ham centre; an attractive appetiser or to serve with drinks.

8 eggs
a little stock or consommé
¼ cup/2 oz/50 g sugar
pinch of salt
ham for filling

Mix all the ingredients except the ham, to make a thin omelette mixture and cook in a pan with a little butter until firm. Place a cubed length of ham across the centre of the omelette and roll the omelette firmly round this. Remove from the pan and chill in roll form until firm. Slice thinly across the roll and arrange the pieces on the serving plate.

Sushi

serves 4

These can be made with tuna fish and avocado. If seaweed sheets are available they can be rolled around the rice, fish and avocado to make round slices. Without seaweed the ingredients can be piled on each other in a small mound.

1–2 avocado
4–6 oz/125–175 g tunafish (preferably raw)
½ cup/4 oz/125 g rice (Japanese or pudding)
rice vinegar
sugar to taste

Scoop out the avocado and slice very thinly. Cook rice in boiling salted water to cover. Drain well, and form into small 1 in/2½ cm diameter rounds. Top with a slice of avocado and piece of tuna fish matching in size. Sprinkle with a little rice vinegar mixed with the sugar to moisten. If sheets of seaweed are available layer rice, avocado and tuna on top of each other on the seaweed and roll up the seaweed, chill and slice into neat rounds. The sushi should be served with a bowl of soy sauce with green radish paste, for dipping.

Pork Ginger (Buta Shoga Yaki) *serves 4*

1½ cups/½ pint/275 ml soy sauce
*1¼ cups/½ pint/275 ml cooking wine
(Japanese or a sweet white wine)*
7 oz/200 g grated ginger root
*8 thin slices pork (each about 4 oz/125 g
in weight*

Mix the soy sauce, ginger and wine in a pan adding a little sugar if a sweeter mixture is preferred. Cook the pork meat gently in this and serve with the cooking liquid as a dipping sauce.

Tempura Seafood and Vegetable *serves 4*

8 Gulf shrimp (or more large prawns)
4 oz/125 g slices of salmon
*slices of egg plant, green pepper, onion,
carrot and mushroom*
for batter:
2½ cups/1 pint/575 ml water
1½ cups/5 oz/150 g flour
2 egg yolks
salt, pepper
vegetable oil for deep-frying

De-shell shrimp leaving a tail-piece of shell on. Peel and slice vegetables thinly. Make a batter by mixing quickly (5–6 stirs only) the water, flour, egg yolks and seasoning and dip seafood and vegetable pieces in the batter. Deep-fry in vegetable oil until crisp and puffy. Serve with fried vegetables and rice, and with a dipping sauce made from a little fish stock combined with soy sauce, cooking wine, a little sugar and salt to taste.

On the QE2 all the correct ingredients, from 20 lb of seaweed or Japanese green radish, to Chinese cooking wine or 40 pumpernickel loaves, are ordered ahead and picked up in good restocking ports like Los Angeles. Singapore, Cape Town, Sydney, Honolulu and Hong Kong are other prime storing ports and dairy produce will be flown from Sydney to Singapore and melons and other fruits from California to Hong Kong. The chef is an expert in what is best and in season all around the world. Orders for the World Cruise in January, initially go out to suppliers in the previous July. In storing the ship, the chef works with the Food and Beverage Manager, Gordon Phillips. He and Chef Bainbridge are on the quayside at each port checking each food consignment; rejecting oranges as too dry, eggs as too stale and making sure all is as perfect as possible. They carry vicious looking, long, thin–bladed knives which cut into sacks, twist out samples of pineapple flesh, and prod other fruits. Like the chef, Gordon Phillips knows as well as a canny housewife how fruit should look. 'Bananas are best with brown spots', he says, 'these are always the sweetest tasting.' One should feel the base of an avocado to see if it 'gives' and is ripe. Pineapples should be golden in colour for perfect dessert eating. Gordon Phillips started his sea life in 1952, as a commis waiter in the kitchens of an old oil tanker where he was sea-sick. He gave up the sea for a while before joining Cunard as a wine and bedroom steward. He has worked in every department of the hotel side of the ship and was once complimented that he 'was making a good job of that, son' while cleaning the main staircase of the former *Queen Elizabeth* — the speaker was General Eisenhower.

The largest of the ship's restaurants is called the Tables of the World and is divided into five sections, with appropriate decor and colour schemes, from the bleached umbrellas with Parisian food shop prints and a thousand-dollar photo blow-up of a Paris scene, to pagodas and bamboo-frame chairs for the Chinese area. In addition there are Italian (with Pucci hangings), Spanish, and British sections with menu ideas to compliment the decor and many passengers order recipes to fit their table surroundings.

The ship visits many Spanish speaking countries both on World and Mediterranean cruises and this **Arroz Con Pollo** recipe is popular and has been served to the port agents in Acapulco.

Arroz Con Pollo   *serves 4*

1 chicken *salt, pepper* *bay leaf* *2 onions* *(continued)*	Cut up the raw chicken and remove meat from bones. Place bones, skin, etc, in water with salt, pepper, bay leaf and 2 chopped onions and simmer to create a good chicken stock. Brown the pieces of chicken

vegetable oil to cook
3 small diced onions
3 peeled and de-seeded tomatoes
2 diced green peppers
1 diced red pepper
1 crushed clove of garlic
1 bay leaf
4 strands saffron
4 oz/125 g diced ham
3 oz/75 g sliced chipolata or other small
   cooked sausage
1 cup/8 oz/225 g rice

meat in vegetable oil. Remove and place on one side. Add to the pan, the onions, tomatoes, peppers, garlic, bay leaf, saffron and seasoning and cook in the vegetable oil and chicken juice until tender but not browned. Place in a casserole with the chicken pieces and add ham and sausage and the rice. Cover with chicken stock and cook in the oven for about 30 minutes at 350F/180C/Gas 4 until the liquid has been absorbed. Remove the bay leaf and press the mixture into a mould or cups and turn out on a serving platter. The outside of the moulded shapes can be garnished with diamond-shaped pieces of pepper and surrounded by peas and asparagus tips. Top the mould with a small amount of coulis, made by dicing finely 1 onion, 1 garlic clove and 2 seeded, peeled tomatoes and cooking gently together.

Chicken Breast Albufeira   *serves 5–6*

Another chicken and rice recipe, this time from Mediterranean cruising to Portugal.

¾ cup/6 oz/175 g butter
3 large chicken breasts, split in half,
   skinned and boned
salt, freshly ground black pepper
⅛ cup/1 oz/25 g finely chopped shallots
3 tbs/45 ml cognac
2½ cups/1 pint/575 ml heavy (double)
   cream

Heat two-thirds of the butter in a large pan and add the chicken breasts seasoned with salt and pepper. Cook over a moderate heat until breasts are browned slightly. Turn them and let them 'stew' in the butter and juices; cover and cook for 10–15 minutes. Do not overcook. Remove chicken to a warmed dish and cover with foil. Keep chicken warm while making the sauce and preparing the rice (see below). Add shallots to the pan and cook briefly. Add cognac and cook for about half a minute. Stir in the cream and cook, stirring frequently, until thickened slightly — about 10 minutes. Season to taste and swirl remaining butter around in the skillet. Spoon the prepared rice onto a large serving dish and make a base for the chicken pieces. Place chicken on the rice and spoon the hot sauce over the meat, keeping most of the sauce to serve separately in a sauce boat.

Albufeira Rice

¼ cup/2 oz/50 g butter
1 tb/15 ml finely chopped onion
½ tsp/2.5 ml minced garlic
1 cup/8 oz/225 g uncooked rice
½ bay leaf
1½ cups/12 fl oz/350 ml chicken stock
salt
4 oz/125 g chicken livers, cut in cubes
1½ cups/12 oz/350 g diced raw
  mushrooms
2 black truffles (optional)
4 pimentos

Preheat oven to 350F/180C/Gas 4. Melt half the butter in an ovenproof saucepan or casserole with a lid. Add the onion and garlic and cook without browning. Add the rice and bay leaf and cook, stirring, for about 2 minutes. Add the stock and salt to taste and bring to the boil. Cover closely and cook for exactly 17 minutes. Meanwhile melt the rest of the butter in another pan and add chicken livers. Cook, stirring, over a moderate heat until the livers lose their red colour. Add the mushrooms and cook until most of the liquid evaporates. Do not overcook or the livers will become too dry. Garnish the chicken pieces with diamond shapes cut from the pimentos and truffles. Chop the remaining pimentos and truffles and when the rice is cooked, remove the bay leaf, and stir in the liver and mushroom mixture, pimentos and truffles.

Still on the Mediterranean cruise circuit, the ship may visit Moroccan ports like Tangier when this version of **Cous Cous** is served with a lamb, beef or chicken stew.

Cous Cous

8 lamb cutlets
4 large pieces chicken
8 oz/225 g chopped rump beef
oil to cook
2 oz/50 g barley
2 oz/50 g chick peas
6 oz/175 g any type of squash
1 turnip
2 leeks
2 carrots
1 head of celery
4 artichoke bottoms (fresh)
1 tsp/5 ml each of cumin, turmeric, salt,
  pepper and saffron
2 oz/50 g diced shallots

In a large heavy pan, fry the meats in the oil until sealed and browned. Add all the vegetables cut in large pieces, with seasoning and enough liquid to simmer gently to a stew consistency without sticking to the pan. Stir frequently.

Cous Cous Grain: soak 10 oz/275 g of cous cous grain with 1¼ cups/½ pint/275 ml chicken stock and after the stock has been absorbed by the grain, spread it out on a large dish and leave to dry. Then steam for 15 minutes, transfer to a pan and shake well, adding some vegetable oil and heat again in the steamer.

Indian chefs come aboard when the ship visits Bombay or Madras but all through the year, the serving of curry at lunchtime is becoming more popular. It is served complete with a tray of crisp, wafer thin poppadum, and a range of condiments such as desiccated coconut, chopped apple and mango chutney. A list describing 38 different curries is carried on board; everything from **Agra** (made with Jerusalem artichokes) to **Zanzibar** (made with sheep's heads and peas). In between comes **Kandahar of Beef,** with coconut; **Lord Clive of Beef,** with apple and ginger and **Lucknow,** duck with tomatoes and green peppers. The ship uses Sharwoods curry spices from a City of London firm established for a century as spice importers.

Derrick Leigh in the Queen's Grill will often, on World Cruises, present curry in a hollowed out pineapple shell for effect. When the whole ship is served the following curry dish, the larder cooks have to get busy boning out 800–900 chicken legs.

Curried Chicken   *serves 4*

1 chicken
bay leaf
salt, pepper
1 onion
butter or oil to cook
for Curry Sauce:
2 onions
2 carrots
2 apples
⅛ cup/2 oz/50 g sultanas
1 banana
½ orange
butter to cook
3 tbs/45 ml curry powder
½ tb/7 ml flour
5 cups/2 pints/1 litre chicken stock
juice of 1 lemon or lime
1 tb/15 ml crushed garlic
1 tsp/5 ml tomato purée
2 tbs/30 ml desiccated coconut
Serve with:
1 cup/8 oz/225 g rice

Cut up a raw chicken removing all the meat from the bones. Cook the bones, skin, etc with water, bay leaf and chopped onion, salt and pepper to make 5 cups/2 pints/1 litre chicken stock. Lightly cook the chopped chicken meat in butter or oil and put on one side. In a big heavy pan make the curry sauce by chopping onions, apples, carrots, sultanas, banana and orange together and lightly cooking in butter until softened but not browned. Add curry powder and flour and stir in until blended as for a roux and add the chicken stock. Gradually bring to the boil, stirring, until thickened and simmer for about 1½ hours. Then add the lime or lemon juice, chopped mango chutney, garlic, and tomato purée and desiccated coconut. Pass through a strainer or blender and place the chicken pieces in a casserole. Cover with the sauce and place in the oven for about 40 minutes at 350F/180C/Gas 4. Boil the rice in boiling salted water for about 17 minutes, covered and serve with the chicken curry.

Chinese dishes are among the most popular and the ship carries plenty of woks and its own set of Chinese stir-fry ideas. A Chinese inspired dish, **Imperial Chop Suey** was chosen as the main dinner dish on the menu of September 20th, 1967 which marked the *Queen Mary's* thousandth transatlantic crossing and last westbound voyage, and the launch of the QE2. This dish comprises diced pork and duckling with julienne vegetables, cooked with molasses and served with Chinese rice and crisp noodles.

Braised Spare Ribs with Pineapple   *serves 6*

2 lb/1 kg pork spare ribs
¼ cup/2 oz soy sauce
½ cup/4 fl oz/125 ml pineapple juice
¼ cup/2 oz/50 g sugar
½ cup/2 fl oz/50 ml vinegar
½ cup/4 fl oz/125 ml water
2 tbs/30 ml oil
1 tb/15 ml flour
½ tsp/2.5 ml salt
1 cup/8 oz/225 g canned pineapple
    pieces
1 tb/15 ml cornstarch (cornflour)
3 tbs/45 ml water

Cut ribs apart and chop each, with the bone, into 2 in/5 cm sections. Add soy sauce and toss pieces in this. Leave to stand in soy sauce for 45 minutes turning occasionally. Drain and discard sauce. Drain canned pineapple and use the juice to combine with sugar, vinegar and water. Heat oil in a heavy pan or wok and add ribs and stir-fry until brown; about 3–4 minutes. Stir in the flour and then the pineapple juice mixture. Heat quickly, then simmer, covered, until ribs are tender; about 45 minutes. Add salt, and pineapple, stirring in gently and to heat through only. Meanwhile blend cornstarch and water to a paste and stir into the sauce to thicken.

Stir-fried Scallops with Ginger Root   *serves 4–6*

Ginger is now much hailed as a cure for sea-sickness and the crystallised ginger in bowls set outside the grill rooms after meals aids digestion a lot.

1 lb/450 g scallops
2 or 3 slices fresh ginger root
1 scallion (spring onion) stalk
½ tsp/2.5 ml salt   *(continued)*

Cut the scallops in quarters or slices if large. Mince ginger root, and cut scallion in 1 in/2½ cm sections. Blend cornstarch and cold water to a paste. Heat the oil, add salt, then ginger root and scallions. Stir-fry a

**One of the five sections of the
Tables of the World Restaurant.**

1 tb/15 ml cornstarch (cornflour)
4 tbs/60 ml water
2 tbs/30 ml oil

few times, add scallops and stir-fry until cooked through; 2–3 minutes. Stir in the cornstarch to thicken and serve at once. For variations, 1 or 2 diced green peppers can be added with the scallops, or 8 oz/225 g sliced mushrooms and for the cornstarch paste, 2 tbs/30 ml soy sauce and 1 tsp/5 ml sugar can be substituted.

Stir-fried Pork and Pineapple   *serves 4–6*

8 oz/225 g lean pork
1 green pepper
1 oz/25 g water chestnuts
2 oz/50 g sweet mixed pickles
2 or 3 slices canned pineapple
1 tb/15 ml cornstarch (cornflour)
2 tsp/10 ml soy sauce
1 or 2 tsp/5–10 ml sugar
3 tbs/45 ml water
2–3 tbs/30–45 ml oil
½ tsp/2.5 ml salt
½ cup/4 fl oz/125 ml stock

Slice the pork thin, cutting against the grain. Slice the green pepper, water chestnuts, and sweet mixed pickles. Cut pineapple slices into chunks. Blend cornstarch, soy sauce, sugar and cold water to a paste. Heat oil, add salt, pork, and stir-fry until pork begins to brown; about 3 minutes. Add green pepper and stir-fry until softens; about 2 minutes. Add pineapple, water chestnuts and sweet pickles and stir-fry for 1 minute more. Stir in stock and heat quickly. Stir in cornstarch to thicken and serve at once.

Desserts include this **Pineapple Seychelles,** invented by John Bainbridge when the QE2 first visited Mahé, the islands' capital.

Pineapple Seychelles   *serves 1*

1 small pineapple, halved
1 oz/25 g desiccated coconut
1 oz/25 g chopped crystallised ginger
dash of Grenadine
for meringue:
4 egg whites
¼ cup/2 oz/50 g sugar
⅓ cup/2 oz/50 g desiccated coconut

Halve the pineapple and scoop out the flesh and dice in small pieces. Mix fruit with coconut, ginger and Grenadine, and replace in the pineapple shell. Make a meringue with the egg whites, sugar and coconut beaten together until stiff. Pipe or pile the meringue over the pineapple and brown under a hot grill.

Salzburger Nockerln   *serves 4*

5 egg whites
½ cup/4 oz/125 g caster sugar
2 egg yolks
½ cup/2 oz/50g flour
vanilla essence   *(continued)*

Beat the egg whites and caster sugar together until stiff in a firm meringue mix. Mix together egg yolks, flour, vanilla essence to taste, lemon and orange rinds and gently fold into the meringue mixture. Mix together the butter, cream and honey, with rum to

grated rind of 1 lemon
grated rind of 1 orange
2 tbs/30 ml butter
⅕ cup/2 oz/50 g cream
⅛ cup/2 oz/50 g honey
rum or rum essence

taste, and place this mixture in the bottom of a greased and sugared soufflé dish. Drop big peaks of the meringue mix on top and bake for 10 minutes at 400F/200C/Gas 6. The meringue will rise in high peaks during cooking and should be served immediately.

Finally, one can finish a meal with Indian or China, or Earl Grey teas, or various coffees.

Turkish Coffee

to make 1 cup

¾ oz/18 g finely ground coffee
¾ oz/18 g sugar
½ cup plus 2 tbs/¼ pint/150 ml water
two drops rosewater

Mix coffee, sugar and water in a copper pot (traditionally one with a long handle) on a heater. Bring to the boil and boil until mixture is frothy. Remove from heat until the froth has subsided and put back on the heater and repeat for a total of three times. To get the coffee grounds to settle add a little cold water and finish with the addition of a few drops of rosewater. Drink without milk.

6 SWEET ELEGANCE
Desserts and Puddings

As well as the many flambé fruits, ice-creams and crêpes described in Chapter 4, the QE2 has a reputation for soufflés and around 300 are served every evening. The confectioners under the direction of Chief Confectioner, Vic Day, from Manchester, keep two basic soufflé mixes, each made from 10 pints of milk, at the ready then cook the soufflés in a careful rotation system as the orders come through so that they arrive at the table puffy and in the best condition.

Basic Soufflé *serves 5*

This is the basic soufflé mix used on the *Queen Elizabeth 2.*

½ cup plus 2 tbs/¼ pint/150 ml milk
½ cup/2 oz/50 g flour
¼ cup/2 oz/50 g butter
¼ cup/2 oz/50 g sugar *(continued)*

Boil the milk with half of the sugar. Make a paste of the butter and flour and stir this into the milk when it is boiling. Stir well until the mixture is thick and leaves the sides of the pan clean. Remove from the

4 eggs
flavouring as required

heat and allow to cool. Separate the eggs and stir the yolks into the mixture. Beat the whites and the rest of the sugar until very stiff and then fold into the mixture. (Required flavourings should be added before folding in the egg whites). Cook at 350F/180C/Gas 4 for about 20 minutes for 1 large, or 10 minutes for individual soufflés. The soufflé mould should be lined with butter and dusted with granulated sugar before the mixture is put into it for cooking.

Of the many soufflé flavours served with tangy fruit and creamy vanilla flavoured sauces, chocolate is the most demanded.

Queen's Chocolate Soufflé *serves 4*

¼ cup/2 oz/50 g butter
¾ cup/3 oz/75 g flour
½ cup plus 2 tbs/¼ pint/150 ml milk
4 egg yolks
3 oz/75 g melted chocolate
4 egg whites
¼ cup/1 oz/25 g caster sugar
for sauce:
4 oz/125 g dark chocolate
½–¾ cup/4–6 oz/125–150 g heavy
(double) cream

Melt the butter in a pan and stir in the flour until smooth and blended. Add milk and bring to the boil stirring well to make a thick sauce. Add the egg yolks off the heat and beat in well. Fold in the melted chocolate and then the egg whites and caster sugar beaten to a stiff mixture. Drop the mixture into individual, or one large, greased and sugared soufflé dish(es) and bake in a moderate oven (350F/180C/Gas 4) for about 20 minutes. Serve with chocolate sauce.

To make sauce: Melt the chocolate in a basin over hot water and stir in the cream until the desired consistency is reached and serve with the soufflé.

For a more special occasion there is the ship's **Soufflé Grand Marnier** served with a sauce made with apricots and more Grand Marnier.

Soufflé Grand Marnier

serves 4

¼ cup/2 oz/50 g sugar
½ cup plus 2 tbs/¼ pint/150 ml milk
¼ cup/2 oz/50 g butter
1½ oz/37 g flour
4 eggs
Grand Marnier to flavour

Boil the milk with half the sugar, mix butter and flour to a paste and stir into the boiling milk and continue to stir until the mixture is thick and smooth and leaves the sides of the pan cleanly. Remove from heat and allow to cool. Separate the eggs and stir yolks into the mixture. Beat egg whites with the rest of the sugar until very stiff. Add Grand Marnier to taste to the main mixture and fold egg whites into mixture. Grease and dust with sugar 1 large or individual soufflé mould(s), fill with the mixture and place in a pan containing ½ in/1 cm water and cook at 350F/180C/Gas 4 for 20–25 minutes (10 minutes for individual soufflés). Serve with an apricot and Grand Marnier sauce made by simmering 1 small can apricot halves in syrup without stones. Allow to cool; blend until smooth and add Grand Marnier to taste. Reheat and serve with the soufflé.

Storing for just a ten day transatlantic trip, the QE2 loads plenty of fresh fruit including 3,000 grapefruit, 15,000 oranges, 6,000 apples, 1,000 melons, 5,000 lemons, 2,000 limes and 2,000 lb grapes as well as 2,500 lb of frozen fruit. On World Cruises soft fruits are the chef's biggest supply headache, while exotic fruits are picked up as the ship travels round. During the 1983 cruise the fruits of Bali were pre-ordered — mangoes, mangosteen, papaya, passion fruit, salak (known as 'snake food') and rambutan.

Poached Pineapple

serves 6

1 fresh pineapple
¼ cup/2 oz/50 g sugar
½ cup/4 fl oz/125 ml sherry
½ cup/4 fl oz/125 ml water
1½ cups/12 oz/350 g redcurrant jelly
½ cup/4 fl oz/125 ml cognac or kirsch
6 portions vanilla ice-cream   *(continued)*

Remove the skin and cut the pineapple into paper thin slices and cut these in half. Mix sugar, sherry and water and bring to the boil in a pan. Poach the pineapple in this mixture for about 5 minutes. Melt the redcurrant jelly over a low heat in another pan and add the drained pineapple and simmer while spooning

macaroon crumbs to garnish

the jelly over the fruit. Cook for about 5 minutes. Add the cognac or kirsch and let it heat for 5 minutes without stirring. When cognac is heated, flame the spirit and spoon over the fruit while it is still burning. Serve this fruit sauce over the vanilla ice-cream and scatter macaroon crumbs on top.

Drunken Apples
serves 2

While flaming in liqueur gives this dish a touch of luxury, the basic ingredient is the humble baked apple.

1 dessertspoonful/10 ml redcurrant jelly
lemon juice
2 cooking apples
kirsch to flame
fresh grapefruit and orange segments
cream and glacé cherries to decorate

Melt the redcurrant jelly in a pan with a little lemon juice to taste. Meanwhile bake the peeled and cored apples in the oven until tender. Place each apple in an ovenproof serving dish and coat with the redcurrant jelly. Flame the fruit with a goodly measure of kirsch and top with orange and grapefruit segments and finish with a swirl of heavy (double) cream and top each apple with a glacé cherry.

Strawberries Romanoff
serves 4–6

1¼ lbs/575 g strawberries
juice and grated rind of 1 orange
juice and grated rind of 1 lemon
½ cup/4 fl oz/125 ml dry curacao
sugar to frost glasses
1¼ cups/½ pint/275 ml whipped cream

Soak the strawberries in the juices of the orange and lemon and the curacao for at least an hour and arrange the fruit in tall glasses which have had the rims frosted with sugar. Top the glass with whipped cream. On the QE2 the cream used is never sweetened, which is a good point for those on a diet.

Banana Bourdaloue Tart
serves 4–6

1 shortcrust flan case about 9 in/22½ cm
    in diameter
4 bananas   *(continued)*

To make the Frangipane mixture: cream together the butter and sugar. Add eggs and beat thoroughly. Add the flour and almonds mixed together, but do not

The Columbia Restaurant.

1²/₃ cups/12 oz/350 g Frangipane
    mixture (see below and right)
2 oz/50 g flaked almonds
1 oz/25 g butter
icing sugar
½ cup plus 2 tbs/¼ pint/150 ml kirsch
    flavoured syrup (kirsch added to a
    sugar [75%] and water [25%]
    mixture and boiled until syrupy but
    clear).
for Frangipane:
½ cup/4 oz/125 g butter
½ cup/4 oz/125 g caster sugar
2 eggs
¼ cup/1 oz/25 g flour
3 oz/75 g ground almonds

overbeat when the flour has been absorbed into the mixture. Place half of the Frangipane mixture over the bottom of the cooked flan case and arrange the bananas, peeled, split in half lengthways, and poached in the kirsch flavoured syrup until tender, on top of this. Cover with the rest of the Frangipane mixture. Sprinkle with flaked almonds and dust with icing sugar and sprinkle with a little melted butter. Bake in a hot oven at 450F/230C/Gas 8 and serve with the hot syrup as a sauce.

Bananas Brazilian Style

serves 6

6 medium bananas
½ cup plus 2 tbs/¼ pint/150 ml fresh
    orange juice
1 tb/15 ml fresh lemon juice
¼ cup/2½ oz/62 g brown sugar
pinch salt
2 tbs/30 ml butter
1⅔ cups/10 fl oz/275 g grated fresh
    coconut (desiccated can be used but
    the result is not nearly so good and
    juicy)

Preheat the oven to 400F/200C/Gas 6. Peel the bananas and cut them lengthways into halves. Place in a buttered casserole. Mix orange and lemon juices, sugar and salt, and pour over the bananas. Dot with butter. Bake for 10–15 minutes then remove from the oven. Before serving, sprinkle bananas with the coconut.

Peach Surprise

serves 6–8

3¾ cups/1½ pints/¾ litre sour cream
½ tsp/2.5 ml nutmeg
1 tsp/5 ml vanilla essence
2½ fl oz/62 ml Grand Marnier or
    Cointreau
1¼ cups/10 oz/275 g light brown sugar
2½ cups/20 oz/550 g peach slices,
    sweetened to taste and flavoured to
    taste with Grand Marnier.

Mix sour cream, nutmeg, vanilla essence, and Grand Marnier. Beat lightly until well blended and pour into a 9 in/22½ cm pie-plate. Sprinkle with the brown sugar and place under a preheated grill. Grill until the sugar caramelises but do not allow to burn. Chill mixture and serve with the peach slices.

Old English Lemon Flummery

serves 4–6

This dessert is suitable for those on a diabetic diet (the ship will provide any kind of diet requested).

2 lemons
2 sheets leaf gelatine
4 eggs
½ cup/4 oz/125 g sugar
½ cup plus 2 tbs/¼ pint/150 ml heavy
    (double) cream

Grate the rind of the lemons and squeeze out the juice. Gently warm juice and dissolve the pre-softened gelatine in the warmed juice. Separate the eggs. Whisk the egg yolks with the sugar until light and creamy. Add to the gelatine. Whip the egg whites until they are very stiff and in peaks. Whip the cream until stiff and then very gently fold cream, followed by the egg whites, into the gelatine mixture. Serve chilled in tall frosted glasses with the rim decorated with a thinly sliced fresh lemon wedge.

Classic dessert recipes also appear frequently on the dessert menus.

Cold Zabaglione

serves 4–6

*½ cup plus 2 tbs/¼ pint/150 ml
    Marsala wine*
½ cup plus 1 tb/5 oz/150 g sugar
12 egg yolks
*5 sheets leaf gelatine (less than 1 oz/25 g
    of powdered gelatine equivalent)*
*½ cup plus 2 tbs/¼ pint/150 ml
    whipped cream*
2½ oz/62 g grated dark chocolate

Whisk together egg yolks, Marsala and sugar. Add gelatine pre-soaked in cold water to cover for 5 minutes before use. Shake excess water off before adding. Whisk mixture until thick in a basin over boiling water. Allow to cool in individual moulds or tall glasses before topping with whipped cream and decorating with grated chocolate. Serve with ladies' fingers biscuits.

Charlotte Russe

serves 4–6

10 sponge fingers
¼ cup/2 oz/50 g caster sugar
2 egg yolks
½ cup plus 2 tbs/¼ pint/150 ml milk
1 vanilla pod
4 sheets leaf gelatine
1 cup/8 oz/225 g whipped cream
angelica and glacé cherries to decorate

Line a greased mould with the sponge fingers and mix together the egg yolks, sugar, milk and vanilla pod. Beat gently in a bowl over hot water until the mixture becomes thick and creamy. Soak the gelatine in cold water to cover for 5 minutes, drain and add to the mixture. Remove vanilla pod and carefully fold in whipped cream. Pour mixture into the sponge-lined mould and leave to set in a cool place. When mixture is set, unmould and decorate with angelica shapes and glacé cherries.

Crème Brulée

serves 4–6

5 eggs
1¼ cup/½ pint/275 ml milk
1¼ cups/½ pint/275 ml cream
¼ cup/2 oz/50 g caster sugar
⅓ cup/3 oz/75g brown sugar

Whisk together the eggs, milk, cream and caster sugar. Pour into a greased mould and bake in a moderate oven at 350F/180C/Gas 4 for about 30 minutes. Allow to cool. Sprinkle brown sugar over the top and allow to caramelise under a hot grill until melted and bubbling but do not allow to burn. Chill and serve cold. This recipe is said to have originated in one of the old Cambridge colleges in England and has the delicious contrast of the crisp, hard, sweet topping and the creamy cool base.

Occasionally the liner has a touch of the British nanny's nursery food on the dessert menu. There's a **Rusk Custard Pudding, Trifle** (which Chef Bainbridge has demonstrated on American TV), creamed rice pudding variations and this traditional winter English pudding.

English Roly-poly Pudding serves 4–6

3 cups/12 oz/350 g flour
4 oz/125 g chopped beef suet
¼ oz/1.5 ml salt
½ oz/13 g baking powder
⅛ cup/1 oz/25 g sugar
1 cup/8 fl oz/225 ml water
12–16 oz/350–450 g raspberry jam

Mix flour, suet, salt, baking powder and sugar together. Add the water gradually and mix gently to make sure the pastry does not toughen. Roll out the suet pastry into an oblong about 6 by 9 in/15 by 22½ cm. Spread the pastry to within ½ in/1 cm of the edges with the raspberry jam. Brush the edges with beaten egg mixed with a little milk and roll up as for Swiss roll. Wrap the roll in greased and floured muslin cloth (the mixture will stick and leave a 'skin' on foil or paper). Tie the ends firmly and steam for 1½ hours. When cooked, leave to cool and slice. Serve with the remainder of the raspberry jam heated in a small pan until hot and smooth.

Chocolate Cream Pie serves 4–6

2½ cups/1 pint/575 ml milk
¾ cup/6 oz/175 g sugar
2½ oz/62 g cornstarch (cornflour)
6 eggs, separated
¾ cup/6 oz/175 g melted chocolate
1½ oz/37 g gelatine
½ cup plus 2 tbs/¼ pint/150 ml
*   whipped cream*
crushed rusks

Boil the milk and mix the cornstarch with egg yolks and half of the sugar. Stir this mixture into the milk off the heat. Mix melted chocolate with the gelatine and beat well. Beat the egg whites with the remainder of the sugar until stiff. Fold the egg whites into the mixture with the whipped cream. Grease a pie-plate and cover the bottom with crushed rusks. Pour the cream mixture on top and chill until set. Decorate as required with whipped cream and chocolate curls.

Good Morning

CHILLED JUICES
Your choice of
Orange – Grapefruit – Pineapple – Prune – Tomato
V8

Chilled Grapefruit – Melon in Season – Baked Apples
Compote of Kadota Figs and Prunes
Assorted Fresh Fruits in Season

CEREALS
(served with cream or milk)
ed Oats – Hominy Grits – Bran Flakes – Raisin Bran
Rice Krispies – Frosted Flakes – Special 'K'
Shredded Wheat – Corn Flakes – Alpen

Clear Onion Soup with Parmesan Cheese

EGGS
Fried – Turned – Poached – Scrambled – Boiled

YOUR SELECTION OF:
American and Danish Bacon
Wiltshire and American Sausages
Broiled Tomatoes

FISH
Broiled Scotch Kippered Herrings
Poached Finnan Haddock in Milk

FROM THE GRILL
(Please allow 15 minutes)
Grilled Lamb Chops
Sauteed Idaho Potatoes

COLD BUFFET
Baked Ham   Sirloin of Beef   Roast Chicken   Roast Turkey
Herring Fillet   Sour Cream   Swiss or Philadelphia Cream Cheese

Lettuce and Tomato   Radishes   Celery Sticks
Spring Onions

FRESHLY BAKED THIS MORNING:
Croissants   Danish Pastries   Brioche   Scotch Baps
White and Graham Rolls   Toast

Honey   Marmalade   Preserves

Pancakes or Buckwheat Cakes with Golden Pancake Syrup

Full Roast Coffee   Instant Coffee   Non-Caffeine Sanka
Ceylon and China Tea   Fresh Milk   Hot Chocolate
Horlicks

Bonjour

LES JUS DE FRUITS
amplemousse – Ananas – Prunes
Tomates – Légumes

amplemousse – Le Melon Frappé
Pomme Au Four
ompote de Figues et Prunes
Basquette de Fruits Frais

LES CÉRÉALES
(au lait ou a'la crême)
miny Grits – Bran Flakes – Raisin Bran
es – Frosted Flakes – Special 'K'
l Wheat – Corn Flakes – Alpen

oupe À L'Oignon Gratinée

LES OEUFS
oché – Brouillés – À'La Coque

CHOIX DE BACON
ericaine ou D'anois Bacon

ucisses Anglaise ou Americaine
Les Tomates Grillées

LES POISSONS
ed Scotch Kippered Herrings
L'Aigrefin Fumé Poché

LES GRILLADES
(15 minutes)
a Chop D'Agneau Grillée
es Pommes Sautées Idaho

LE BUFFET FROID
L'Aloyau de Boeuf – Le Poulet Rôti
Le Dindonneau Rôti
g À L'Huice – Les Fromages Fins
t Tomates – Les Radis – Le Celeri
es Oignons du Printemps

LES PAINS
ts – Le Pain D'Anois – Les Brioches
ais – Les Petits Pains – Le Pain Grillé

LES CONFITURES
– La Marmelade – Les Confitures

de Blé ou Naturelle, Servis Au Sirop

LES BOISSONS
afé – Le Néscafé – Le Sanka
he et de Celon – Le Lait – Le Chocolat
Horlicks

Morgen

FTE UND FRÜCHTE
h – Ananas – Pflaumen
en – V8

Melone (saison bedingt)
n oder Pflaumen Kompott
saison bedingt)

CKENGERICHTE
oder sahne serviert)
merikanische Gries-Speise)
Rosinen – Rice Krispies
l 'K' – Shredded Wheat
s – Alpen

mit Parmesan Käse

PEISEN
ier – Rühreier – Setzeier
te Eier

SIE WÄHLEN:
r Dänischem Speck
Englischen Würstchen
Tomate

RICHTE
e Von Schottland
ilch Gedünstet

RILL
ezeit erlauben)
eletten
offeln

ÜFFET
Rostbeef – Gebratenes
– Herings Fillet in Saurer
Philadelphia Weichkäse
Radieschen – Sellerie
ngszwiebeln

CKSTUBE
Backwerk – Brioche
isse und Braune Brötchen
st

de Konfitüre

Hellem Syrup

NKE
– "Instant" Kaffee
eylon und China Tee
kao – Horlicks

Dias

S
DE
seca Tomat
Manzanas
a y Prunos
stación

leche)
Copos de s
asas
Especial T
lpén'

eso Parmesá

tos Pasado

DE
danés
le Wiltshire
o

horno
da en leche

minutos)
a parilla
eadas

llo asado
a amarga
iladelphia
Apio Ceb

he Bollos
Tostadas

con almiba

cafeinado
a Chocola

7 A THOUSAND EGG EYE-OPENER

Breakfasts and Brunches

The *Queen Elizabeth 2* gets through a thousand eggs every breakfast (4,000 a day) and drinks half a million cups of coffee during a World Cruise. William Chambers noted steak and hock for breakfast in the early Cunard days and in the 'twenties it was said that only snobs drank a second bottle of champagne before breakfast. Breakfasts are no longer as flamboyant as they were; boar's head was on the *Queen Mary's* breakfast list until 1967, and Ron Pitcher says the days of the champagne breakfast are almost over.

But even today, the trend towards lighter Continental-style breakfasts among all passengers is tempered by the temptations of a still substantial menu. The list is printed in four languages: English, French, German and Spanish while the Japanese have their own separately printed menus for which the waiters carry a pocket translation. It includes all the basic styles of egg, chilled juices (6), and a fruit selection including melon, baked apples, compote of figs and prunes and fresh fruit salad. There are ten cereals including rolled oats for the Scots and Hominy

Grits for deep Southerners. Bacon, sausages, tomatoes, kippers, poached finnan haddie (smoked haddock fillet), grilled lamb chops with sautéed potatoes, and a cold buffet which includes sirloin of beef, ham, roast chicken and turkey, herring fillet with sour cream, Swiss or Philadelphia cream cheese and salads will keep body and soul together until lunchtime.

Then there are the baked goods, including pancakes or waffles freshly made that morning and served with honey, marmalade and preserves.

In the grill rooms, a young waiter wheels round a trolley of rolls, brioches, croissants, Danish pastries, muffins and other breads and at least eight different marmalades (the QE2, after all, comes from Scotland and 800 dozen jars of marmalade are carried on each transatlantic crossing), three or four English preserves and two or three honeys. To wash all this down there is a choice of various coffees and teas, milk, hot chocolate or Horlicks.

On the 1983 Pacific Cruise, the ship almost had her chance to make her own honey. A swarm of bees complete with queen, who obviously fancied living off another Queen, came on board during the Panama Canal transit. The swarm settled happily under one of the umbrellas around the aft-deck pool which meant that the deck had to be closed to passengers while a sample bee was caught and sent ashore for identification at Balboa. It was found to be an African bee; part of a swarm which had escaped from a breeding programme in Brazil, moved to Peru and which was now making its way towards the States. The queen was isolated and sent ashore with the rest of the bees during the evening.

English Muffins *makes 8–10*

A traditional recipe from Britain now almost lost there, but popular in the USA.

3 cups/12 oz/350 g flour
1 tsp/5 ml salt
¼ cup/2 oz/50 g butter
2 tbs/1 oz/25 g sugar
½ oz/12 g yeast
1½ cups/12 fl oz/350 ml water
beaten egg mixed with a little milk

Rub the sieved flour, salt, butter and sugar together. Mix the yeast and water together and when frothy knead into the dough mix. Allow the dough to rest for about 10 minutes then knead again. Mould into bun rolls and place on a greased baking sheet. Leave to prove, until double in size. Flatten with the palm of the hand and brush with beaten egg mixed with a little milk and bake in a preheated oven at 425F/250C/Gas 7 for about 10 minutes. Turn the muffins over on the baking sheet and cook for a further 5 minutes. The muffins are usually served cut in half and toasted, spread with butter and jam and can be eaten at breakfast or, as traditionally in England, for afternoon tea.

Brioche
makes 6–8

1½ cups/6 oz/175 g flour
½ cup/4 oz/125 g butter
2 eggs
¾ oz/18 g sugar
½ oz/12 g yeast

Beat together the flour and butter. Mix together the eggs, sugar and yeast in a separate bowl. Leave for about 10 minutes for the yeast to prove. Mix in the flour and butter and knead until smooth. Place pieces of the dough in greased moulds (individual foil cases can be bought in packets and used). Leave until the dough rises over the top of the moulds (keeping in a warm place) and then bake in the oven at 375F/190C/Gas 5 until risen and golden brown.

Corn Muffins
makes about 8

1½ oz/37 g sugar
¼ cup/2 oz/50 g shortening (lard)
1 egg
4 oz/125 g cornmeal
1½ cups/6 oz/175 g flour
½ oz/12 g baking powder
1¼ cups/½ pint/275 ml milk

Beat together the sugar, shortening and egg. Add in the flour and baking powder and mix with the milk to make a dough that is smooth and flowing but not runny. Place spoonfuls of the mixture in greased bun pans or foil cases as above and bake in the oven at 375F/190C/Gas 5 for 20 minutes. The corn muffins are best served hot with lots of butter.

If your hangover is a little heavy, then the ship will soothe it with this soup served every day for breakfast.

French Onion Soup

serves 4

3 cups/12 oz/350 g sliced onions
¼ cup/2 oz/50 g butter
¼ tsp/1.5 ml mixed herbs
5 cups/2 pints/1 litre chicken stock
grated Parmesan or Gruyère cheese
salt, pepper

Cook the onions gently in a big pan with the melted butter, stirring occasionally, until the onions are softened but not browned. Add the herbs, seasoning and chicken stock. Cook, simmering, for an hour and reduce the liquid until it is thick with onion. Serve in bowls with plenty of grated Parmesan or Gruyère cheese on top. On the QE2 this is served with croûtons of French bread fried in butter and sprinkled with Parmesan cheese.

Sausages are not made on the ship as the skins are not carried. But the ship has a good recipe for a sausage mixture which can be served in patty form for breakfast, or for a brunch party.

Savoury Sausage

serves 4

¾ lb/350 g loin of pork meat
¼ lb/125 g veal
¾ cup/3 oz/75 g breadcrumbs or rusk
    meal
1 tsp/5 ml mixed herbs
1 egg
salt, pepper
butter or oil to fry

Grind (mince) the pork and veal very finely and mix in the breadcrumbs, herbs and egg; blending well until smooth and even. The mixture can be put into sausage skins if they are available; if not, shape the meat into small patties on a floured pastry board and fry gently on a low heat until cooked through and browned.

Salmon Fishcakes

serves 4

This recipe is very much enjoyed at breakfast by the ship's doctor.

8 oz/225 g tinned salmon
4 oz/125 g mashed potatoes (cooked
    boiled potatoes, seasoned, and
    creamed with a little milk or cream
    and butter until fluffy)
1 tsp/5 ml chopped parsley
2 egg yolks
salt, freshly ground black pepper
flour to dust
2 eggs
2 tbs/30 ml milk
2 cups/8 oz/225 g white breadcrumbs
vegetable oil to cook

Mix together the salmon, mashed potatoes, parsley with the egg yolks, salt and pepper. Form into a ball and then shape in flat, round cakes about 2 in/5 cm in diameter. Lightly dust the cakes with flour. Beat the eggs with milk and dip the fishcakes in the mixture and roll in white breadcrumbs. Fry in deep vegetable oil until golden brown. The salmon cakes can also be shallow-fried, carefully turning until cooked through and can be served with tomato sauce.

Recently a new dimension to breakfast has been added to the QE2 with the extension of her lido deck. With a covered deck area and a new kitchen, a basic breakfast of egg and bacon variations can now be served there. But there are many breakfast and brunch dishes which are available on request either at breakfast or on the lunch menu for late risers. These, like the ones below, can be copied as light supper dishes, as can the ship's savouries detailed in Chapter 9.

Farmer's Rarebit

serves 4

1 lb/½ kg grated cheddar cheese
½ cup plus 2 tbs/¼ pint/150 ml basic
    white sauce (made with ⅛ cup/1 oz/
    25 g butter mixed with ¼ cup/1 oz/
    25 g flour and blended on a gentle
    heat with the milk and stirred over
    heat until thick and seasoned to taste)
½ cup plus 2 tbs/¼ pint/125 ml strong
    beer
¼ tsp/1.5 ml mustard
1 tsp/5 ml Worcester sauce
2 egg yolks
1 oz/25 g sliced, cooked mushrooms
1 oz/25 g sliced strips of ham
1 tsp/5 ml cooked, chopped onion
salt, freshly ground black pepper

In a double boiler mix the cheese into the hot white sauce and add mustard, Worcester sauce and beer and stir until smooth and all the cheese has melted. Add salt and pepper to taste and remove from the heat. Off the heat, stir in egg yolks and blend until smooth. Prepare large rounds of buttered toast for each person and arrange sliced, cooked mushrooms, ham and onion on the toast. Pour the cheese mixture over the top. On the ship this is served with grilled tomatoes and Lyonnaise potatoes.

Egg Petit Duc

serves 1

2 eggs
a little grated horseradish
2 oz/50 g cooked, diced mushrooms
salt, freshly ground black pepper
tomato ketchup to taste

Butter a small ovenproof serving dish and break the eggs into the dish. Round the eggs, arrange mushrooms on top and scatter on the grated horseradish mixed with the tomato ketchup. Season to taste. Cook in a moderate oven (350F/180C/ Gas 4) for 5 minutes until the eggs are set.

Scrambled Eggs Magda

serves 1

2 eggs
1 oz/25 g grated cheddar cheese
¼ tsp/1.5 ml hot mustard
¼ tsp/1.5 ml chopped parsley
1 tsp/5 ml diced toast or fried bread
butter to cook
a little cream
salt, freshly ground black pepper

Scramble the eggs in a little melted butter and season to taste and add a little cream (about 2 tsp/10 ml) to soften the eggs. Mix in the cheese, mustard, parsley and diced toast and cook until heated through. Serve immediately with extra slices of butter toast.

Morning Omelette

serves 1

2 eggs
a little cream
salt, freshly ground black pepper
1 oz/25 g diced fried potatoes
1 oz/25 g diced ham
butter to cook

Melt the butter in an omelette pan; break in the eggs and season. Cook the omelette as normal and scatter on potatoes and diced ham; fold over and serve at once.

Crabmeat Royale

serves 4

8 oz/225 g flaked crabmeat
1 tsp/5 ml chopped olives
1 tsp/5 ml chopped shallots
4 tsp/20 ml chopped red and green
      pepper
salt, freshly ground black pepper   *(cont)*

Mix together the crabmeat, chives, shallots, peppers and seasoning to taste and place in a buttered ovenproof dish. Cover with the cheese sauce made by melting the butter and stirring in the flour to make a paste and then blending over a gentle heat with the

**The Deck Buffet:
hamburgers and frankfurters.**

for Creamy Cheddar Cheese Sauce:
1 oz/25 g butter
¼ cup/1 oz/25 g flour
1¼ cups/½ pint/225 ml milk
½ cup minus 1 tb/4 oz/125 g grated
*   cheddar cheese*
1 tb/15 ml Worcester sauce
4 tbs/60 ml dry white wine

milk until smooth and thickened. Season to taste and add the cheese and stir until it has all melted. Add the Worcester sauce and the white wine. Bake the crabmeat with the sauce on top in a moderate oven (350F/180C/Gas 4) for 5–10 minutes until browned on top.

Turban of Chicken Livers Orientale *serves 4*

8 oz/225 g chicken livers
½ cup/4 oz/125 g butter
⅔ cup/4 oxz/125 g chopped scallions
   (spring onions)
1 tsp/5 ml mixed herbs
salt, pepper
8 tsb/120 ml tomato ketchup
1 cup/8 oz/225 g uncooked rice
1 tsp/5 ml blanched raisins
1 tsp/5 ml chopped almonds

Cook the chicken livers gently in the butter and add the scallions, herbs and seasoning. When cooked (but not overcooked and hard) mix in the tomato ketchup and allow to simmer gently. Meanwhile boil the rice in boiling salted water to cover for 17 minutes, covered. Place chicken liver mixture on a hot serving dish and arrange the rice, mixed with the raisins and almonds, around it. Serve immediately.

Potato Lutkas *serves 4*

This is a potato dish which is served on QE2 at lunch with sauberbraten; a round of beef marinated in vinegar with sliced onions, braised and cooked with raisins and ginger. It is also fine for serving for breakfast or supper with fried eggs.

2½ cups/20 oz/575 g grated, peeled raw
   potato, dried on kitchen paper
⅓ cup/2 oz/50 g chopped onion
4 eggs
2 tbs/30 ml flour
salt, freshly ground black pepper
vegetable oil to cook

Beat all the ingredients together until a thick mix is obtained and everything clings together. Spoon into a shallow frying pan and cook in vegetable oil until very crisp and brown on both sides. Serve immediately.

Cornish Pasties *makes 8*

A traditional pastry dish taken to work by Cornish miners. It was said that the pastry would withstand being dropped down a mine shaft. In hard times only a little vegetable was put in the pastie, and there is a saying that the devil would never go to Cornwall for fear he would be put in a pastie. The QE2's tasty filling includes plenty of beef as well as vegetables.

for the pastry:
6 cups/1½ lb/675 g flour
1⅛ cups/9 oz/250 g shortening (lard) or margarine
1 tb/15 ml salt
¼ cup/2 oz/50 g water (enough to bind for a rough pastry)
for the filling:
3 lbs/1½ kg top round or topside cut of beef
2 cups/12 oz/350 g diced onion
2 lbs/1 kg diced potatoes
1¼ cups/10 oz/275 g diced carrots
1 tb/15 ml salt
pepper
½ tsp/2.5 ml chopped parsley

Make the pastry by rubbing together the flour, and salt with the shortening. Bind to a rough pastry with cold water; adding more as necessary. Put pastry on one side in a cool place. Make the pastie filling by simmering the beef cut into ¼ in/½ cm cubes, in a large pan, letting the meat sweat its juices out on a gentle heat. When meat is just sealed, add the vegetables diced very small (about ⅛ in/¼ cm in size) and stir round. Cook gently, covered, in their own juices. Add seasoning to taste and chopped parsley, and stir well. Meanwhile roll out the pastry on a lightly floured board and cut in circles about 5 in/12½ cm in diameter (a large saucer or small plate can be used as a guide). Place equal spoonfuls of the meat mixture in the centre of each pastry circle and seal the edges pressing firmly together and crimping to decorate. Brush with a little milk or beaten egg to get a good glaze and bake at 350F/180C/Gas 4 for about an hour until golden brown. Hot or cold Cornish pasties make excellent picnic as well as brunch fare.

Chicken and Ham Croquettes   *serves 4*

3 oz/75 g butter
2 tbs/30 ml flour
1¼ cups/½ pint/275 ml milk
1 cup/8 oz/225 g finely diced cooked chicken
1 cup/8 oz/225 g finely diced ham
2 egg yolks
salt, pepper
for egg wash:
1 egg
4 tbs/60 ml milk
flour to dust   *(continued)*

Melt the butter in a pan and mix in the flour to make a paste. Gradually add the milk, stirring well, and bring to the boil, stirring, until the sauce has thickened and is smooth. Remove from the heat and allow to cool. Add to the sauce, the chicken and ham and put through a blender until a thickish paste is obtained (it should not be too smooth). Add the egg yolks and season to taste beating in well. Shape mixture into cylinders about 2 in/5 cm long and about 1 in/2½ cm thick. Dip the cylinders in the beaten egg mixed with the milk and then dust the croquettes lightly with

2 cups/8 oz/225 g white breadcrumbs
vegetable oil to fry

flour. Add the breadcrumbs to the remains of the egg wash and roll the croquettes in this. Fry in vegetable oil until golden brown all over. The croquettes should be served with green peas and tomato sauce.

Cumberland Veal and Pork Cakes *serves 6–8*

4 cups/2 lb/1 kg finely ground (minced)
    veal
2 cups/1 lb/450 g finely ground (minced)
    pork
2½ cups/1 pint/575 ml cream
1 tsp/5 ml chopped parsley
½ tsp/2.5 ml freshly ground black
    pepper
1 tsp/5 ml salt
2 finely minced onions
4 eggs
½ cup/4 oz/125 g butter
1¾ cups plus 2 tbs/¾ pint/425 ml light
    (single) cream
½ tsp/2.5 ml tomato purée
salt, pepper
1 tsp/5 ml cornstarch (cornflour)

By hand or in a blender, mix together the veal, pork, parsley, onions and seasoning with the cream and eggs; beat well until mixture forms a rough paste and sticks together (the meats should be uncooked). Form the mixture into flat cakes with floured hands or on a floured board. Melt the butter in a frying pan and brown cakes on both sides to seal in the juices. Place in an ovenproof dish and cook in the oven at 350F/ 180C/Gas 4 for 30 minutes until cooked through. When cooked, brown off in a shallow pan with a little melted butter. Remove to a serving dish and keep hot. Add the cream to the frying pan and mix in with any juices and add to tomato purée and seasoning to taste. Mix well and simmer until thickened or add the cornstarch dissolved in a little water. Just before serving pour the cream sauce over the meat cakes and serve at once. Chef Bainbridge suggests serving the cakes with small tablespoonfuls of mashed parsnips.

For brunch times, **Cheese Soufflé** is very popular with those watching their weight or planning a special order dinner. **Eggs Benedict** is a traditional American brunch favourite and can be served on a base of **English Muffin** (see page 94).

Eggs Benedict *serves 1*

1 English muffin (see page 94)
2 poached eggs   (continued)

Butter the English muffin split in half and place a slice of ham on each half and top each half with a poached

2 slices ham (preferably the sugar-cured
    type)
2 slices truffle (optional, as very
    expensive)
for the Hollandaise Sauce:
3 egg yolks
1 dessertspoonful/10 ml malt vinegar
2 cups/1 lb/450 g unsalted butter, melted
    and warm
salt, freshly ground black pepper
juice of ½ lemon

egg. Cover with the Hollandaise Sauce which is made by whipping in a double boiler (the mixture must never be allowed to boil) the egg yolks and vinegar until very thick. Remove pan from heat and gradually add in the warm, melted butter whisking rapidly. If the sauce becomes too thick, a little warm water can be added to keep it to the right consistency. Finish the sauce by seasoning to taste and adding in the lemon juice. Place truffle slices if used (or a sliced black olive for decoration) on top of the sauce on each egg and brown quickly under a hot grill.

8 FIVE MEALS A DAY

Buffets and Afternoon Teas (and Petit Fours)

On transatlantic crossings, midnight snacks are served in the bars and savouries added to the dinner menus. On World and Caribbean cruises, there are elaborate midnight buffets and, when the weather is warm, midday buffets served from stainless steel serveries by waiters wearing white gloves. The recently added kitchen and covered Club Lido deck area extends the area of deck buffets.

Hamburgers and frankfurters are also served on deck on cruises and eaten round the aft-deck swimming pool with iced tea. Daily records of hamburger consumption are kept; 270 a day were eaten on a fairly brisk weather day at sea. The daily records also noted 200 passengers were on special diets.

The larder cooks do much of the basic preparation for a buffet. Skinning and preparing cold cooked trout for example; decorating the fish's sides with pimento strips and sliced olives and then coating with aspic.

The following is a traditional British recipe which goes well on a buffet table.

Cold Veal-and-Ham Pie *serves 6*

The 'raised' pastry used here is so called because in the old days, before moulds, the pastry oblongs, also once known as coffins, were shaped up by hand rather as a potter shapes a pot. It is an art that is now almost lost in Britain.

for the 'raised' pastry:
2 cups/8 oz/225 g flour
¼ tsp/1.2 ml salt
3 oz/75 g shortening (lard)
3 fl oz/75 ml water
for the pie filling:
1½ lb/675 g lean veal
8 oz/225 g cooked ham
3 hard-boiled eggs
1 tsp/5 ml mixed herbs
1 tsp/5 ml chopped parsley
½ cup plus 2 tsb/¼ pint/150 ml chicken bouillon
salt, pepper

Make the pastry by placing flour and salt in a warm basin and mixing together. Boil water with the shortening for 5 minutes and, with a spoon, mix in with the flour until the mixture is blended enough to be able to knead. Knead well. Allow the pastry to rest for an hour and then knead again. During this time keep the pastry warm, but do not allow it to become too loose. Roll out on a floured board and use (as soon as possible) to line a greased, long, oblong cake tin, or terrine mould with spring release sides. Leave enough pastry to make a covering lid. Meanwhile dice the veal and ham into ½ in/1 cm cubes and mix with herbs, parsley and seasoning, place in a layer in the pastry mould. Place the hard-boiled eggs in a line on top of the meat and add the rest of the meat to fill the mould well. Add the chicken bouillon to moisten. Place the lid of pastry on top and seal well round the edges, crimping into a neat pattern. Make a hole in the centre of the lid and cover with a round 'button' of pastry. Bake in a moderate oven (350F/180C/Gas 4) for two hours. When the pie has been removed from the oven and is almost cold remove the pastry 'button' and top up any space in the pie with aspic jelly (made from chicken bouillon with gelatine added) poured through a funnel into the pie. Serve cold in slices with salad.

On special days such as passing through the Panama Canal, when everyone stays on deck in order that they may not miss a moment of the drama of going through the locks, there is an extra-special deck buffet. For the 1983 Panama transit, whole sucking pigs were roasted and chopped into pieces for service with an array of salads. The centrepiece of the buffet was a whole pig skilfully decorated by the Japanese chef with a tomato flower 'crown'. Onion flowers, made by cutting a large onion in very fine strips down towards its roots, fanning the pieces out and colouring with a little cochineal, and thick circles of cored apple with the centres filled with redcurrant jelly, surrounded the pig.

An idea for the hostess who wants to keep her party dress clean while doing messy chores can be taken from William Soutter, the chef in charge of the ship's buffets. He cuts holes for his neck and arms in a king-size garbage bag and pulls it over his white chef's clothes to keep them clean while he is chopping up items like sucking pig. He comes from Liverpool and has been with Cunard since 1955, working on many of the fleet's ships before joining the QE2 at her launch. He has the wearying job of staying up every night on cruises to supervise the midnight buffet; a superb spread of elegant foods arranged across the rear of the Columbia Restaurant on a buffet which features two of the Janine Janet, mother of pearl and seashell sculptures of the four elements which were originally designed for the Princess Grill. Lights are dimmed and the buffet is often highlighted by a small lit fountain. Soutter reckons to get 300 customers a night on World Cruises and even after a heavy dinner, up to a thousand on the shorter Caribbean cruises. Many of the ship's performers and dancers will come down late and make the midnight buffet their evening meal.

The buffets are not as elaborate in decoration as on the old liners when, on sailing day, hams would be converted to crinolined ladies or have Grenadier Guards outlined in sauce on them; spun sugar evolved into the Liberty Bell or St Paul's Cathedral and rose

Opposite: **Above: The midnight buffet in the Columbia Restaurant.**
Below: The central display of the midnight buffet, with fountain, glazed and decorated hams and icing swans.

bouquets of potato were perfumed with scent. But the skills, if not the time, are still there and Adrian Clover from Crawley in Sussex, who has worked for five years on the QE2, passes on some of his tips for making buffet centrepieces at home.

For decorating meats, Adrian Clover suggests making a Chaud Froid coating from a normal basic béchamel sauce thickened with ½ oz/13 g gelatine dissolved in a little hot water for every 2½ cups/1 pint/575 ml of sauce. The amount of gelatine can be doubled if leaving the decorated food out for some time. In any case, items for an evening occasion should only be prepared the afternoon before and kept in the fridge though it is possible to deep freeze items carefully. Chaud Froid sauces like this should not be put on the day before or they will shrink.

A ham takes about 3¾ cups/1½ pints/850 ml sauce to cover and the coating, which is ladled on, sets quicker if the ham is first chilled in the fridge. For turkeys and chickens, the sauce can be made brown with gravy browning and ½ oz/13 g aspic added to each 2½ cups/1 pint/575 ml of sauce. This much sauce (2½ cups/1 pint/575 ml) will cover six chickens or two turkeys. Once coated with the sauce the meats should be left in the fridge or a cool larder.

When the coating is just on the point of setting, decorative patterns can be added. On a ham, one of the most effective is a bunch of grapes made from sliced black olives, with stalks made of cucumber pieces. A popular QE2 decoration is a tomato rose made by slicing thick pieces of skin from the stalk end of the tomato with a sharp knife. The skin piece is bent round and round flower fashion and fixed in place until set with a piece of cocktail stick. Flower leaves can be made from cucumber or the green leaves of celery.

Whole poached salmon are decorated with olives for eyes and cucumber and radish slices down the back. A sardine or small trout is often placed in the salmon's mouth. Whitebait (very small fish, traditionally in Britain fried and served whole as an appetiser) are set in gelatine coloured to represent water, and arranged round the salmon as if swimming. The salmon can also be presented surrounded by finely chopped gelatine coloured water-blue on the outside and white near the fish to make it look as if swimming.

Two trimmed racks of lamb can be sewn together into a crown shape and the centre filled with a small swede to keep the circular shape during roasting. Before serving, the trimmed bones are decorated with small paper frills and topped with small, cherry tomatoes.

A midnight buffet attraction is the gâteaux table and many people slip down just for a cup of coffee and a slice of gâteaux before continuing dancing, listening to the music, playing the casino tables, or, after the end of the evening film show in the theatre, having a quiet nightcap in one of the bars.

George Day, from Essex, has worked eleven years for Cunard, nine of them on the QE2 and as Chief Baker his department works 24 hours a day. Luckily his cooks on their well stabilised ship don't suffer as did the bakers of Dickens' day. In 1840 Dickens noted on his stormy Cunard crossing, 'The baker is ill and so is the pastry cook. A new man, horribly indisposed, has been required to fill the place of the latter officer and has been propped and jammed up with empty casks in a little house upon deck and commanded to roll out pie crust which he protests (being highly bilious) it is death to him to look at'.

So deck joggers can enjoy an informal dawn buffet and coffee and freshly baked buns and later, one can take afternoon tea at leisure with some of the confectionery and bakery department's offerings detailed below. For the midnight and other buffets and tea, Vic Day, the Chief Confectioner, who worked in catering management ashore before joining the QE2 three years ago, makes gâteaux and pastries. His department also creates special decorative items for occasions like the Christmas buffet where an elaborate gingerbread house may be coated with the ship's varnish to preserve it on display. Cruising in the Caribbean, uneaten

Christmas cake is usually given to poor children on one of the islands.

For the midnight buffet gâteaux tables, traditional **Pecan Pie** is a much liked sweetmeat and this recipe comes from Chef Derrick Leigh.

Pecan Pie

serves 6–8

3 beaten eggs
½ cup plus 1 tb/5 oz/150 g sugar
1¼ cups/½ pint/275 g Golden Syrup or
   a light corn syrup
2½ cups/10 oz/275 g chopped pecan
   nuts
2 tbs/30 ml melted butter
large pinch of salt
unbaked 9 in/22½ cm shortcrust pie shell

Mix all the ingredients together well and pour into the prepared pastry shell. Bake for 35–40 minutes in the oven at 375F/190C/Gas 5.

Pecan Puffs

makes about 50

Another good way of cooking pecans, these make good petit fours served with coffee; another idea from Chef Derrick Leigh.

½ cup plus 1 tb/5 oz/150 g butter
2 tbs/30 ml sugar
2½ cups/10 oz/275 g flour
2½ cups/10 oz/275 g chopped pecans
½ tsp/2.5 ml vanilla essence
½ tsp/2.5 ml salt
caster sugar to coat

Cream together the butter and sugar until fluffy and beat in the flour, nuts, vanilla essence and salt. Mix together with the hands until well blended. Break off small pieces of the mixture about the size of a large marble and roll in the hands until smooth and firm. Arrange on a greased baking sheet and bake for 30 minutes at 325F/160C/Gas 3. While still hot, roll in caster sugar. Allow to cool and when cold, roll again in the caster sugar.

Two gâteaux ideas from Vic Day's department are also featured on dinner dessert menus and buffets.

Hungarian Log

8 eggs
1 cup/8 oz/225 g caster sugar
1½ cups/6 oz/175 g flour
½ cup/2 oz/50 g cocoa powder
2½ cups/1 pint/575 ml whipped cream
6 oz/175 g roasted, flaked almonds
6 oz/175 g pitted black cherries which
    have been soaked in a little kirsch
½ cup plus 2 tbs/¼ pint/150 ml
    whipped cream

In a bowl, whisk together the eggs and sugar and when smooth and creamy so that the whisk marks hold in the mixture, gradually add in the flour and cocoa powder, first sieving them together, and folding in very gently. Spread the mixture out on a greased Swiss roll baking sheet and bake at 375F/190C/Gas 5 for about 7–10 minutes until cooked. Allow to cool. Tip the sponge carefully out of the baking sheet onto a pastry board covered evenly with a thin layer of caster sugar to prevent it sticking. Mix the first amount of whipped cream with the roasted almonds and spread carefully over the sponge. Roll up carefully and decorate along the top of the roll with the second amount of whipped cream and the cherries. Serve in 1½ in/3½ cm slices for tea or as a desssert with chocolate sauce (see page 85).

Gooseberry Gâteau

1½ cups/¾ lb/350 g margarine
1½ cup/¾ lb/350 g caster sugar
6 eggs
2½ cups/10 oz/275 g flour
2 oz/50 g ground almonds
10 oz/275 g firm gooseberries
apricot jam
Bought marzipan to cover (or make from
    a basic mix of 2 parts ground
    almonds to 1 part caster sugar, mix
    together in a basin over boiling
    water. Off the heat work together on
    a cold marble slab really well, but do
    not let the almonds become 'oily').
for 'icing':
¼ cup/2 oz/50 g melted chocolate
6 oz/ 175 g apricot jam
pistacchio nuts to decorate

Cream together the margarine and sugar until fluffy and beat in the eggs. Add the flour and ground almonds. Fold in the gooseberries gently, taking care not to break the fruit. The fruit will sink to the bottom of the mixture during cooking. Place the mixture in a tin about 1½ in/3½ cm deep and about 12 in/30 cm by 2 in/5 cm. Bake in a moderate oven (350F/180C/Gas 4) for 20 minutes. When cooked, allow to cool. When cold, remove from the tin and slice in half lengthways. Sandwich the two halves together with apricot jam; the gooseberries will now make two decorative layers. Trim cake ends and wrap in marzipan and top with an 'icing' of the chocolate and apricot jam heated together in a bowl over boiling water. Spread over the cake and decorate with pistacchio nuts. This recipe is presented in small slices with whipped cream on the lunch menu but can also be served for afternoon tea.

For the traditional British afternoon tea, served daily on the QE2, eight different types of cake (a total of 2,000 cakes) are made each day. Top favourite is chocolate eclair, followed by cold cheesecake and an expensive, very rich, English fruit cake, similar to a wedding cake mix. Tea is taken in the two main public rooms served by girls in tartan kilts. In suitable weather, tea is also served on deck and even in the tropics it is a delight to lie in a steamer chair on the top helicopter deck sipping hot tea with milk or lemon or iced tea in a glass and nibbling a chocolate eclair, racing against the sun to get to the chocolate. On deck, the deck stewards bring small, neat trays carrying individual teapot, jug, and sugar bowl in old Cunard china, square in shape to fit neatly on the tray.

Plain Madeira Cake *makes 2 x 2 lb/1 kg size cakes*

This is a light, almost bread-like cake, somewhat similar in consistency to a pound cake, and is served in slices on the afternoon trays. Leftovers form the base of **Baked Alaska.**

2¼ cups/1 lb 2 oz/500 g sugar
2¼ cups/1 lb 2 oz/500 g margarine
4½ cups/1 lb 2 oz/500 g flour
2 oz/50 g ground almonds
8 eggs

Cream together the sugar and margarine. Gradually fold in the flour, the ground almonds and finally, the beaten eggs. Pour the mixture, which should be smooth and well blended, into greased cake tins and bake in the oven for 2–2½ hours at 375F/190C/Gas 5. Allow to cool in the tins and then on a cake rack.

Cold Cheese Cake *serves 4–6*

1¼ cups/8 oz/225 g cream cheese
2 egg yolks
¾ cup/4 oz/125 g icing sugar
4 sheets of gelatine   *(continued)*

Mix together the cream cheese, egg yolks and icing sugar. Pre-soak the gelatine in water for 5 minutes and drain. Dissolve gelatine in the milk over a gentle heat and leave to cool. Soak sultanas in the rum and

½ cup plus 2 tbs/¼ pint/150 ml milk
1¼ oz/30 g sultanas
¼ oz/6 ml dark rum
pinch salt
½ cup plus 2 tbs/¼ pint/150 ml cream
grated rind and juice of 1 lemon

whip the cream with the salt until stiff. Mix cream, cheese, sultanas, gelatine mix, a few drops of vanilla essence to taste, lemon juice and grated rind together, folding in the whipped cream very carefully. Spread the mixture on a Swiss roll tin, or other shallow tin, about 9 by 6 in/22½ by 15 cm and chill until set. Cut into slices to serve.

Date, Honey and Walnut Cake

makes 3 x 1 lb/450 g cakes

3 cups/¾ lb/250 g flour
¾ cup plus 1 tb/7 oz/200 g caster sugar
1 oz/ 25 ml milk
½ oz/13 g baking powder
⅛ cup/2 oz/50 g honey
5 oz/ 150 g butter
2 eggs
½ cup/4 oz/125 ml water
¼ cup/2 oz/50 g sultanas
½ cup/2 oz/50 g chopped walnuts
6 oz/ 175 g chopped dates

Mix flour, caster sugar, milk, baking powder, honey and butter together to make a loose, crumbly mixture. Mix together the eggs and water in a basin and beat into the mixture until smooth. Add the sultanas, chopped walnuts, and dates to the mixture blending in well. Place in three greased 1 lb/450 g bread or cake tins and bake at 350F/180C/Gas 4 for about 45 minutes–1 hour until a skewer pushed into the cake comes out clean.

Walnut Cake

makes a 3 lb/1½ kg cake or three 1 lb/450 g cakes

1 cup/8 oz/225 g butter
2 cups/1 lb/450 g caster sugar
4 eggs
2 cups/8 oz/225 g flour
⅛ cup/2 oz/50g corn syrup or Golden Syrup
½ cup/2 oz/50 g milk powder
½ cup/2 oz/50 g chopped walnuts
2½ oz/62 ml water
few drops vanilla essence

Cream together the butter and half the amount of sugar with the eggs until smooth. Fold in the flour, syrup, milk powder, the rest of the sugar, walnuts and water. Flavour to taste with a few drops of vanilla essence and put mixture in greased cake tins. Bake in the oven for 45 minutes at 350F/180C/Gas 4 until a skewer pushed into the cake comes out clean.

Victoria Sandwich

One of the personal favourites of Chef John Bainbridge.

½ cup/4 oz/125 g caster sugar
1½ cups/6 oz/175 g flour
2 eggs
½ tsp/2.5 ml baking powder
½ cup/4 oz/125 g margarine
jam for filling
icing sugar to dust

Cream the margarine and sugar together well until soft and fluffy. Gradually add in beaten eggs. Gently fold in the flour and baking powder sieved together. Divide the mixture evenly between two greased 7 in/ 17½ cm sponge tins. Bake in a hot oven at 450–475F/ 230–240C/Gas 8–9 for about 12–15 minutes. Turn out onto a wire rack to cool. Spread one half of the sponge with jam to choice and sandwich with the other half on top. Dust with icing sugar and serve. Chef Bainbridge points out that there are several things that can make a sponge mixture less than perfect. A very close texture means under beating, too much flour, or the oven has been too hot or too cool. If the texture has holes in it, the flour has not been sufficiently folded in or the tin has been filled unevenly. If the crust is cracked the oven has been too hot. If the sponge has sunk, the oven has been too hot or the tin removed from the heat during cooking. If there are white spots on the surface, then the mixture was insuffienctly beaten.

Coconut Layer Cake

½ cup/4 oz/125 g margarine
½ cup/4 oz/125 g caster sugar
½ cup plus 2 tbs/¼ pint/150 ml milk
3 eggs whites
vanilla essence
½ oz/13 g baking powder
1 cup/4 oz/125 g flour
1 cup/6 oz/175 g desiccated coconut

Beat the margarine with the sugar until light and fluffy. Add the milk slowly and the unbeaten egg whites with a few drops of vanilla essence to taste and baking powder sifted with the flour. When well but gently mixed, add in by folding the coconut. Pour mixture into two well greased 8 in/20 cm sandwich tins and cook at 350F/180C/Gas 4 for 35 minutes. Allow to cook on a wire rack and sandwich together with frosting (icing) to choice. Spread frosting on top and sprinkle with coconut to finish.

Chef Bainbridge checks the pastries
and petit fours. A special occasion cake
can be seen in the background.

Edinburgh Shortbread

Served for afternoon tea and with desserts on the special January 25th, Burns' Night menu.

2 cups/8 oz/225 g flour
5 oz/150 g butter
2½ oz/62 g sugar
about ¼ oz/6 g lemon juice
1 egg

Rub together the flour, butter and sugar and when nearly mixed add the lemon juice and the egg. Mix well and roll out mixture onto a ½in/1 cm deep well greased baking sheet and prick well through with a fork and lightly mark out divisions for fingers. Bake in a moderate oven (350F/180C/Gas 4) until golden brown; about 10–15 minutes. When cooked, allow to cool slightly, dredge with caster sugar and break or cut into fingers.

Petit fours are a decorative feature of every dinner served with the coffee and over 3,000 pieces are cut and made each night by Vic Day's confectionery department, and a tray looks well on any buffet table. One of the QE2's confectioners, Stephen Hallam, is nicknamed 'The Petit Four Man' and the **Chocolate Nutty Hallams** below were invented by him and named after him. They are extremely rich but delicious and will defeat any will power not to eat them.

Coconut Galettes

makes about 40

2 cups/1 lb/450 g sugar
2⅔ cups/1 lb/450 g coconut
3 eggs
¾ cup/3 oz/75 g flour

Mix all the ingredients together and put in ¾ in/2 cm mounds on a well greased baking tray. Bake until golden brown at 350F/180C/Gas 4.

Chocolate Nutty Hallams

makes about 12

5 oz/150 g roasted, flaked almonds (cont)

Melt the chocolate over boiling water in a basin and

1 cup/8 oz/225 g sultanas (soaked for at least 8 hours in dark rum)
12 oz/350 g dark chocolate

mix with the almonds and sultanas. Turn onto a wax paper covered baking tray and spread mixture approximately ¾ in/2 cm thick. Chill, and when set, cut into small squares.

Turkish Delight *makes about 50 pieces*

½ cup plus 2 tbs/¼ pint/150 ml orange juice
6 cups/3 lbs/1½ kg sugar
2 drops orange colouring
24 sheets of pre-soaked leaf gelatine
¾ cup/6 oz/275 g cornstarch (cornflour) mixed till smooth with 1 oz/85 ml water
equal mix of cornstarch (cornflour) and icing sugar

Boil the orange juice and sugar to a temperature of 240F. Add the colouring and gelatine and finally the cornstarch. Mix well and pour into a level tray about ½ in/1 cm deep. Chill well until set and cut into ¾ in/2 cm squares and roll in a mixture of equal amounts cornstarch and icing sugar.

Apéritifs

Cinzano (Red or Bianco)
Martini Rossi (Sweet or Dry)
Noilly Prat
Pernod
Dubonnet
Campari
Akvavit
Fernet Branca

Port

Today's Open Port
Vintage Port

Sherry

Sherry, a selection

Spirits

QE2 SINGLE MALT
SCOTCH WHISKY
over 12 years old - E

Blended Scotch Wh
Deluxe Blended Sc
Whisky
Pure Malt Scotch V
Irish Whiskey
Rye
Bourbon
Premium Bourbon
Gin
Rum
Vodka
Russian Vodka

Minerals served as mixe
All liquors served are pr

Mixed

Bloody Mary
Bullshot
Gin Fizz
Screwdriver
John Collins
Negroni
Pimms
Rum Collins
Planter's Pu
Tom Collins
Vodka Coll
Whisky So

Cognac and

Hine Old Vintage Gra
Champagne Cognac
Cognac Napoléon
Cognac VSOP
Cognac ★ ★ ★
Amaretto
Apricot Brandy
Bénédictine
Brandy & Bénédictine
Calvados
Chartreuse
Cherry Heering
Cointreau
Crème de Menthe
Crème de Cacao
Curaçao

Cocktails

Mexicola
Bronx
Everglades Sling
Daiquiri
Gimlet
Harvey Wallbanger
Jack Rose
Martini
Rob Roy
Grasshopper
Side Car
Stinger
Vodkatini
White Lady
Pink Lady
Old Fashioned

Cocktails

Queen Elizabeth 2
Manhattan
Florida Sunrise
Sombrero
Barbados Swizzle
Tequila Sunrise
Afrikander
Bali Hi
Del Rio
Mai Tai
Waikiki Cooler
Seychelles Shaker
Pinacolada
Singapore Sling
Hong Kong Gimblet

CUNARD

Bar List

CUNARD

CUNARD

9 BLOODY MARYS AND SKINNY SOLDIERS
Cocktails, Canapés and Savouries

The *Queen Elizabeth 2* is one of the most glamorous places to give a party. Passengers who go on the World Cruise regularly are great party givers. The occasion of the World Cruise attracts many; one lady has moved to a smaller house, sold her car and other possessions to make that annual voyage, and a New Jersey pantry maid saved for six years to make the trip. Not only can party givers pick happily from literally tons of caviare (2 tons are on board for the World Cruise), paté de foie gras (2,500 tins of best quality Georges Bruck) and endless ideas from the chefs, but they can also make their parties memorable with fresh floral decorations from the ship's own florist. One man had a wall of greenery arranged in the Double Down suite, others have small table posies set out. The florist has some bird cages which are filled with trailing plants and flowers for parties and floral colours will be themed to a special day such as St Patrick's. Flowers are bought from suppliers round the world and kept fresh in a large cooler in the shop until needed. The florist also copes with the mammoth job of changing all the ship's floral displays every six days.

Even the well stocked library near the Queen's Room is haunted by avid party hostesses searching the reference books for ideas for unusual cake shapes. On the 90 day World Cruises, passengers vie with each other to give the most memorable cocktail party. There are a number of areas around the ship which can be used for private parties including the Princess Grill lounge, the Club Lido (formerly the Q4 nightclub designed by David Hicks), the area known as UHMB — Under Her Majesty's Bust — a section of the gold and white Queen's Room around the Oscar Nemon sculptured bust of the Queen of England, and the Double Down suite which acts, during the day, as the social centre and bureau where invitations can be ordered from the ship's printer and help is on hand to write them out and deliver them to cabins.

On one World Cruise, a party to remember was given on what is known as the helicopter deck. This is the highest open deck aft and is shielded by glass screens. The party was held late at night on a beautiful warm evening. A bar and tables for serving hot and cold foods were set up under umbrellas and decorated with garlands of flowers. Potted palms and plants gathered from around the ship gave a garden effect and each lady guest was presented with a rose as she arrived. About 200 guests enjoyed the evening and were entertained by a trio playing music. Singing groups, the Double Down bar's pianist Flo Glenn, and other musicians are often hired by party givers to add to the occasion.

Ann Brooks has been on all nine World Cruises to date and is a great hostess and party giver both at her Californian home and on the ship. Ann gives parties at 11.30pm when her 115–140 guests, including many of the ship's officers, gather in the Club Lido where there is an open champagne bar and conversation to a dance-band background. The party goes on afterwards to the midnight buffet. Ann likes to create party themes and to give each guest a little souvenir which she bases on inspiration at ports of call. One year it was a ceramic monkey to celebrate the Chinese year of the monkey. Another of Ann's party rules on the QE2 is to ask each male guest to dance, at least once, with the lady she introduces him to.

One year, Ann gave a surprise birthday party for the ship's Captain, Doug Ridley (now the Executive Captain) and her recipe for a paté birthday cake has become a prized idea among regular passengers. Ann uses 2 brown Zweiger sausages but soft liver paté sausages could be used instead. These are mixed with 1½ cups/½ pint/275 ml cream cheese into which crumbled Roquefort is added to taste. The flavour of the Roquefort must not dominate the mix. Add Worcester sauce and a little hot mustard to taste with enough mayonnaise to thin the mixture down to a consistency whereby it can be easily spread. The whole is moulded into an oiled cake shape and chilled. When unmoulded, 'Happy Birthday' is 'iced' on top with white cream cheese and it is decorated with candles. The paté cake is served dolloped onto cracker biscuits and serves about 6 people. It's a lovely idea to try for anniversary parties when the honoured guest does not like sweet cakes.

Caviare, of course, is very popular for parties; one man spent over 300 dollars on a 4 lb bowl for his party. The ship gets through about 20 lbs a night and the stores are carefully guarded by a two key system. Deep-fried shrimps, pizzas big and small, quiches, chicken legs, small hot dogs, meat pieces and devilled eggs are other popular party fare. **Egg Rolls** (see page 126) are served bite-sized and scrambled eggs are mixed with a little Roquefort cheese and served on cracker biscuits. One passenger on the 1982 World Cruise brought two of her own ideas to the ship; **Skinny Indians** and peanut butter and bacon on triangles of toast, and they have been swiftly adopted.

For **Skinny Indians,** blend together 1⅓ cup/8 oz/ 225 g creamed cheese with 4 oz/125 g chipped beef or chopped, sliced York ham and 2 oz/50 g scallions (spring onions) chopped very finely. Roll mixture, with a little seasoning to taste, into small fingers and then roll in diced, chipped beef or ham. This makes enough for 10 servings. The other canapé idea is to spread peanut butter on triangular or round pieces of toast and then cover with chopped crispy bacon and chopped walnuts.

Hot Cheese Dip   *makes around 10 small servings*

2½ cups/1 pint/575 ml light (single
    cream)
½ cup/2 oz/50 g flour
2 lb/1 kg grated cheddar cheese
1 tb/15 ml Worcester sauce
2 oz/50 g hot mustard
2 crushed cloves garlic
salt, pepper
dash of Tabasco sauce

Heat the cream. Mix flour and cheese and stir into the heated cream until it thickens and the cheese melts. Add Worcester sauce, garlic, mustard, salt, pepper and Tabasco and stir in until well blended. Serve warm as a dip with fingers of toast made from rye, white or wholemeal bread to dunk in the dip.

Steak Tartare

serves 4 (for main course)/10 (for cocktails)

3 cups/1½ lb/675 g finely ground
    (minced) tenderloin or sirloin steak
    with no fat on it
2 eggs
⅓ cup/2 oz/50 g finely chopped onion
salt, pepper
chopped parsley

Served on the QE2 either as a main course or as an unusual dish at cocktail parties.

Mix all the ingredients well together and form into small round cakes about 1 in/2½ cm in diameter. Serve for cocktail parties on bread rounds decorated with chopped, hard-boiled eggs, capers and grated horseradish. A little brandy can be mixed with the meat mixture if desired. The meat should be mixed only a short time before serving or the meat will become discoloured.

Deep-fried Salmon   *serves 10*

10 oz/275 g tinned salmon
10 oz/275 g freshly made mashed potato
2 eggs   *(continued)*

Mix salmon, potato, eggs and salt and pepper together until smooth and well blended. Mould into 1 in/2½ cm rounds, coat lightly with flour and egg wash (the beaten egg with a little milk). Roll in white

salt, freshly ground black pepper
flour
beaten egg, with a little milk, for coating
white breadcrumbs
vegetable oil for frying

breadcrumbs and fry in the vegetable oil until golden brown and puffy. Drain on kitchen paper and serve decorated with parsley.

Spinach Dip

serves about 10

An economical dip and liked by vegetarians.

1 cup/8 oz/225 g finely chopped cooked
    spinach
2 oz/50 g scallions (spring onions)
1 oz/25 g parsley
1¼ cups/½ pint/275 ml thick
    mayonnaise
a dash of chili sauce
salt, pepper

Drain the spinach extremely well and pat as dry as possible with kitchen paper. Chop the spinach and mix with the scallions and parsley both chopped very fine. Blend with the mayonnaise, add a dash of chili sauce and salt and pepper to taste. Serve the spread on toast fingers or on small, salty, crisp biscuits.

Cheese Dip

serves about 6

⅔ cup/4 oz/125 g cream cheese
1¼ cups/½ pint/275 ml sour cream
dash of celery salt
1 tsp/5 ml soy sauce
2 oz/50 g diced fresh celery
½ oz/13 g chopped parsley

Mix all the ingredients together well until smooth and serve with sliced raw vegetables or biscuits.

The ship makes many varieties of dips for cocktail parties. Simple mixes are 1¼ cups/½ pint/275 ml sour cream mixed with 9 oz/250 g grated blue cheese spiked with a dash of chili sauce and chopped parsley and served with raw vegetable pieces. Mayonnaise can be mixed with sour cream as a base and given flavour with 4 oz/125 g curry sauce or powder and 1 oz/25 g Indian chutney chopped finely and blended in.

Avocado Dip

Another favourite travelling in the tropics.

2 avocados
1¼ cups/½ pint/275 ml sour cream
2 oz/50 g chili sauce
½ oz/13 g diced green chili
salt, pepper

Blend all the ingredients together until smooth, check seasoning, and adjust to taste.

As well as the private parties, passengers will be invited (in two groups, to accommodate all the travellers) to the Captain's cocktail party held every voyage. These parties are held in the Queen's Room or Double Down Room and in addition to the open bar there are big platters of succulent canapés made by Billy Light from Southampton, a larder cook who has been a dozen years on the QE2. In the afternoon when the galley is quiet, Billy puts together around 1,440 canapés for the Captain's parties and on other nights, arranges trayfuls for smaller parties.

There are dozens of ideas for quick party canapés that can be copied from the QE2 and Billy Light. One effective way of using up small amounts of shrimp, lobster or crayfish (or at Christmas time, pieces of turkey and ham) is to make a light, fish or chicken stock and add in some gelatine. Dice the seafood or meat fairly finely, add to the gelatine mix and leave to set in a square mould. When firm, this can be unmoulded and sliced into small squares or cubes and served on toast pieces or biscuits.

Philadelphia cream cheese is a useful base for all kinds of little bite-sized appetisers. It can be rolled in balls with crisp, diced bacon, chopped or pickled walnuts or diced smoked salmon, and rolled in chopped nuts.

When caviare is served on toast, a tip from the QE2 larder is to place a round of hard-boiled egg between the toast and the caviare to stop the toast from becoming soggy. A little finely chopped egg white can be scattered on top of caviare canapés for colour contrast and Cunard serve their caviare in tiny pastry shells which can be bought ready-made.

Mini rolls of smoked salmon are served on toast topped with capers or a black olive, and 1 in/2½ cm pieces of celery are piped full of Roquefort cheese and tipped with a halved glacé cherry for colour. **Black Eyed Susans** are button mushrooms with the stalk removed and the centres piped with the yellow of hard-boiled egg softened with butter, and topped with a slice of a black olive.

Finally, the trays are garnished with radish or tomato flowers. The trick of making the latter, says Billy Light, is to slice a small piece off the bottom of the tomato and cut three-quarters of the way through with a sharp knife. Turn the knife around, turning all the time to produce a thick skin piece shaped like a flower. On the *Queen Mary* there was a man employed to do nothing but put parsley decoration on canapés; the first thing the passengers did, of course, was to remove the parsley.

Hot Cheese Canapés
makes about 12

1 tb/15 ml flour
paprika, pepper
½ tsp/2.5 ml salt
¼ cup/2¼ oz/56 g grated cheddar cheese
2 tsp/10 ml finely chopped or minced
    canned pimento
1 egg white
chopped peanuts
fat for frying

Mix the flour, paprika, pepper, salt, cheese and pimento together. Whisk the egg white until stiff and fold carefully into the mixture. Form into small rounds and roll these in the beaten egg yolk and then in the chopped peanuts. Fry in deep, hot fat until golden brown and puffy. Drain on kitchen paper and serve hot.

Hot Shrimp Canapés
makes about 12

1 lb/450 g finely peeled shrimps
2 minced spring onions   *(continued)*

Stir the minced onion into the finely chopped shrimps and blend with enough mayonnaise to make a thick

mayonnaise to blend
12 small circles of toast
paprika

mixture that holds together. Spread on the toast, piling the mixture up a little in the centre. Sprinkle with paprika and place under a hot grill until sizzling. Serve at once.

Egg Rolls

makes 6 large, 18 small

for pancake mixture:
2 eggs
1¼ cups/½ pint/275 ml milk
¾ cup/3 oz/75 g flour
for filling:
butter for cooking
1 green pepper
1 red pepper
1 medium onion
2 oz/50 g shrimp
4 oz/125 g canned bean sprouts
2 oz/50 g diced, cooked chicken breast
1 oz/25 g diced ham
1 oz/25 g cooked green peas
1½ fl oz/37 ml soy sauce
salt, pepper
flour to dust
beaten egg
white breadcrumbs
vegetable oil for cooking

Make the pancakes by beating together eggs and milk and then blending in the flour. Cook gently in a small pan making them small and thin, stacking them up ready for use. Make the filling by dicing the peppers, onion and shrimp small, and tossing lightly in butter in a pan. Add the bean sprouts, chicken, ham and peas and season with the soy sauce and salt and pepper to taste. Lightly mix all these ingredients together then spoon equal amounts into each prepared pancake and roll up. Dip each pancake in flour and then beaten egg and roll in freshly made white breadcrumbs. Deep-fry in vegetable oil until golden brown.

Quiche Alaska

serves about 10–12 cut in small fingers; 4–6 as a main course

a 9 in/22½ cm prepared shortcrust flan
case
¼ cup/2 oz/50 g chopped green pepper
⅓ cup/2 oz/50 g chopped onions
2 oz/50 g mushrooms
butter to cook
3 eggs
1¾ cups plus 2 tbs/¾ pint/425 ml milk
oregano
salt, pepper
1 cup/6 oz/175 g diced Alaskan king
crabmeat

Prepare a shortcrust pastry flan. Finely dice and cook in butter, the green peppers, onions and mushrooms and mix with the beaten eggs and milk. Add the oregano and salt and pepper to taste. Add in the cooked crabmeat and pour the mixture into the pastry case. Cook for about 25–30 minutes in a moderate oven (350F/180C/Gas 4) or until mixture is firm.

A cocktail party tray of canapés.

The following are some traditional savouries.

Scotch Woodcock

serves 1

3 eggs
1 tb/15 ml light (single) cream
salt, pepper
butter to cook
slice of bread
anchovy fillets to garnish
capers to garnish
paprika to garnish

Beat the eggs with the cream and season to taste. Melt the butter in a pan and beat in the eggs and cream and cook until scrambled. Toast a round croûton of bread and spread with the scrambled egg. Top with anchovy fillets, capers and finish with a dash of paprika.

Croque Monsieur

serves 1

Sandwich a slice of Gruyère cheese between two slices of ham and buttered white bread. Press firmly together. Cut the sandwich into fingers and dip the fingers in beaten egg mix with a little cream and fry until crisp and golden in a little butter.

Welsh Rarebit

serves 2

½ cup minus 1 tb/4 oz/125 g grated cheddar cheese
1 egg
pinch mustard powder
1 dessertspoonful/10 ml Worcester sauce
salt, freshly ground black pepper

Mix the cheese and egg together and add the Worcester sauce and mustard powder and season to taste. Heat through gently, stirring well, in butter in a pan and when cheese is melted and smooth spread over rounds of toast and serve at once.

Other traditional savoury ideas which also make suitable cocktail party fare are **Canapé Derby, Canapé Diane** and **Croûte Windsor.** For the first, spread a round of toast with finely diced ham blended with finely chopped mango chutney to taste. Top with a sliced pickled walnut. For **Canapé Diane** spread creamed smoked finnan haddie (smoked haddock fillet beaten to a smooth paste with cream, and salt and pepper to taste) on a round of toast, top with a slice of cheddar cheese and place under the grill until the cheese melts and is browned. **Croûte Windsor** is a paste of creamed ham spread on a toasted round of bread and topped with small fried mushrooms.

But you do not have to give a party to enjoy the liquid delights of this ship. One can sip a long, cool tropical drink of the daytime like a Pina Colada, or a bright and refreshing Buck's Fizz (orange juice and champagne) while on deck soaking up the sun. Or one can meet friends in one of the seven bars. The crew have five bars of their own with plenty of draught beer. Bars are chosen by mood and time of day. The Double Down Bar is a morning bar, as is the Club

Lido with its good view of the deck. In the evenings people head for the Double Down Bar for piano music by Flo Glenn. The Theatre Bar is for late swingers while the Casino Hideaway Bar, with its quiet beiges and greenery, is for quiet tête à têtes. The Midship's Bar is where the Columbia Restaurant diners meet before meals and the officers gather after dinner. The lights glow dimly in brass naval lamps on the green and black decor and a classical guitarist or pianist will sometimes play. Outside are tables bearing giant jigsaws of over 4,000 pieces to which passers-by add a piece or two on their way to and from the bar or become totally hooked. The Queen's Grill diners have their own elegant, blue silk and sycamore wood, corridor-style, lounge bar.

No one is likely to drink the ship dry. Clive Jackson, the Head Barkeeper and his men see to that. Clive Jackson has been at sea for 32 years and joined the QE2 on Clydeside. He is responsible for stocking the ship with drinking and smoking supplies. For a World Cruise two million cigarettes are carried and he also copes with making sure each bar has the 2,000 lb of ice needed on a single hot day.

His cellar stock for the World Cruise (enough for 100 days) is so vast as to be almost unbelievable. Extra space is found in the car holds, which have special chilling facilities, for the 10,300 bottles of champagne (18 varieties of French including Cunard's house champagne, Ritz; and US varieties, as well as 2,250 half bottles), 10,400 bottles of red wine and 21,600 bottles of white wine, as well as half bottles; 36,000 minerals, 16,500 bottles of beer, plus 18,000 gallons draught, 4,500 bottles gin, 1,950 brandy and cognac, 10,600 Scotch whisky, 11,000 Bourbon, 1,000 rye, 160 Irish whiskey, 4,100 rum and 1,960 bottles of assorted liqueurs all well insured against storm damage.

The 6,600 bottles of vodka are much needed, as Bloody Marys, with variations of Screwdriver, and vodka and tonic are the ship's favourite drinks having taken over from the old gin-and-tonic and scotch-and-soda routine. Even so, 41 brands of whisky are still carried. Michael Woodleigh, from Liphook in

Hampshire, barkeeper of the Midship's Bar has been 7 years in this bar. He says the Midship's Bar follows the traditions of the *Queen Mary* and the *Queen Elizabeth,* and attracts the cocktail set from 11am until after dinner. Special drinks are created for different ports of call on cruises and for occasions like royal weddings.

This ship has her own malt whisky and her own cocktails. The QE2 cocktail is a blend of 1½ oz/62 ml cognac; ½ oz/13 ml sweet vermouth, 1½ oz/62 ml orance curacao, a dash of Grenadine and lemon juice to taste. It is shaken well and served chilled. For the ship's tenth anniversary in 1979, another cocktail was devised in the QE2's honour. This mixes two-thirds Bourbon with one-third peach brandy, flavoured with lemon juice and Grenadine with a dash of Angostura bitters and served on the rocks.

Among the cocktails and long drinks served on cruises are the following ideas.

Batida

2 oz/50 ml rum
grapefruit juice
pineapple juice
1 banana
dash of Grenadine
a little honey
grated coconut
almond essence
cracked ice

Place all the ingredients in a blender using equal amounts of pineapple and grapefruit juice to taste, the banana, chopped in small pieces, and honey to sweeten. Mix for 1 minute, strain into a tall chilled glass and decorate with a cherry.

Barbados Swizzle

juice of ½ lime
1 tsp/5 ml sugar
4 dashes Angostura bitters
2½ oz/62 ml rum

Place the ingredients in a tall glass and add 2 spoonfuls of shaved ice. Shake well until the mixture foams and serve topped with club soda.

Volcano Cocktail

½ oz/13 ml vodka
6 dashes rum
2 oz/50 ml Southern Comfort

Shake the ingredients together with ice and strain into a glass. Serve with a twist of lemon peel on top.

Seychelles Shaker

Mix together equal amounts of white rum and Cointreau, and add lemon juice and Grenadine to taste. Place in tall glasses and top with soda.

Bombay Cocktail

¼ oz/6 ml sweet vermouth
¼ oz/6 ml dry vermouth
3 dashes curacao
2 oz/50 ml brandy

Mix all the ingredients together and shake with ice and strain into a glass.

Kandy Cooler

juice of ½ lemon
2 dashes Grenadine
¼ measure apricot brandy
¼ measure gin
¼ measure Calvados

Shake the ingredients together well. Strain into a tall glass and top with soda water. Decorate with fruit.

Hong Kong Gimlet

powdered sugar
2 oz/50 ml gin
lemon juice

Put sugar, gin and lemon juice in a cocktail shaker with plenty of cracked ice. Shake well, strain and pour into a cocktail glass until about two-thirds full. Fill with carbonated water and serve ice cold.

Japanese Fizz

juice of ½ lemon
1 tsp/5 ml powdered sugar
1½ oz/37 ml Bourbon
½ oz/13 ml port wine
white of egg

Shake the ingredients together well with cracked ice. Strain into a highball glass and fill with carbonated water and stir. Serve with a slice of pineapple.

Yokahama Cocktail

1 dash Pernod
⅙ Grenadine
⅙ vodka
⅓ orange juice
⅓ dry gin

Shake ingredients together well and strain into a cocktail glass.

Los Angeles Cocktail

juice of ½ lemon
1 tsp/5 ml powdered sugar
1 egg
¼ tsp/1.2 ml sweet vermouth
1½ oz/37 ml Scotch whisky

Shake ingredients together and strain into a cocktail glass.

The QE2 also has her own refreshing and non-alcoholic fruit punch and plenty of non-alcoholic mixed drinks and mineral waters. In addition, some bars, when tropical fruits are available, will feature some of the Golden Door health drinks such as the following:

Grapefruit Mint Frappé   serves 4

6 oz/175 ml unsweetened grapefruit
    concentrate
1 cup/4 oz/125 g fresh grapefruit sections
ice cubes
6–8 mint leaves

Blend together the ingredients and serve in a tall glass.

Cranberry Apple Frappé

serves 4

1 cup/8 fl oz/225 ml cranberry juice
1 cup/8 fl oz/225 ml unfiltered apple
    juice
1 apple, cored and chopped up
1 cup/8 fl oz/225 sparkling water
ice cubes

Blend all the ingredients together and serve.

Banana Smoothie

serves 4

1 ripe banana
1 cup/8 fl oz/225 ml fresh orange juice
1 cup/8 fl oz/225 ml unfiltered apple
    juice
1 cup/8 fl oz/225 ml sparkling water
ice cubes

Blend all the ingredients together and serve with an orange wedge and sprinkled with cinnamon.

And if you do have too happy an hour the night before, the barkeepers are ready with their remedies to soothe the over emotional stomach. Michael Woodleigh swears by the ship's 'Stabiliser' cure, an equal mix of port wine and brandy. Fernet Branca is taken straight with a glass of water on the side, though Americans like to soften the blow to the taste buds by mixing it with green crème de menthe. The number one drink, Bloody Mary also settles a lot of morning-after problems. Clive Jackson says parsley water is a known cure for an upset stomach, now rarely used, and there was a barkeeper on the *Queen Mary* who supped a teaspoonful of olive oil and garlic each day to keep fit and healthy.

The Ritz

* * *

Lunch-time

Cream of courgette and cucumber with fresh dill
———
Fresh salmon mousse in puff pastry with shellfish sauce
———
An artichoke bottom with minced mushrooms and maltaise sauce

* * *

Roast loin of pork with seasoned pudding and mustard vinegar
———
A casserole of monkfish, with seasonal vegetables
———
An Irish stew
———
Served with purée potatoes and buttered cabbage

* * *

Bread and butter pudding
———
Orange and lemon syllabub with a fruit purée
———
Lemon meringue pie

* * *

10 PUTTING ON THE RITZ

The Cuisine of the Shore Sister

The Ritz Hotel in London's Picadilly is owned, like the QE2, by Trafalgar House. One of the grandest tours available in the twentieth century is to travel on the QE2 from New York to Britain, stay at the Ritz for a week with a chauffeur-driven limousine for sightseeing, and then return home by Concorde.

Passengers who stay at the Ritz, or the Bristol, a neighbouring hotel in the same group, are transferred from Southampton by special coach and the Ritz Hotel, under its general manager, Michael Duffell, hosts a champagne reception for passengers at which, of course, the Ritz champagne is served (as on the *Queen Elizabeth 2*). The hotel has chosen three Epernay-produced champagnes to bear its name, a pink champagne, a non-vintage and a 1973 vintage.

Behind the concierge's desk in the rotunda entrance to the hotel on Arlington Street, hangs a board giving QE2 sailing information and the Bureau on the ship will make mid-ocean reservations on request, for the Ritz and other Cunard hotels in Britain: the Bristol, the Cunard International in

London and the Cambridgeshire near Cambridge. The marketing of hotels on ocean liners is nothing new. Cesar Ritz himself thought of it. He was very friendly with architect Charles Mewes, who, at the turn of the century, was creating stately home ambiences on the great liners. Ritz asked Mewes to help design his London hotel which was to be the first steel-frame building in London. Building began in 1904 and it was opened in 1906. Much later, when Trafalgar House, the Cunard holding company, took over the hotel in the mid-1970's, and carried out an extensive programme of refurbishment and updating, Sir Dennis Lennon, one of the designers on the original QE2 team and still a consultant designer, did some of the special bedroom designs and was influenced by Mewes' work. Another QE2 designer, the man who outlined the gracious yacht lines of her decks, was Jon Bannenberg, who also created some Ritz designer bedrooms and used striking nautical themes in his suites which include decorative ship models and impressive mirror effects in the bathrooms.

Mewes liked to recreate Louis XVI settings and the Ritz Hotel recalls what the interiors of some of the QE2's ocean ancestors must have looked like in their opulence and gilded finery. Cesar Ritz, son of a Swiss peasant who became known as 'the hotelkeeper of kings and king of hotelkeepers' had definite views on what he wanted in his hotels. He wanted the Ritz to be as much a home from home for his princely and noble clients as possible, with lots of space and comfort. He was very fastidious about hygiene and was a pioneer in putting private bathrooms in hotels. He disliked wallpaper, heavy drapes, wardrobes and wooden beds because they attracted dust. His original brass bedsteads still gleam in many of the rooms in the Ritz and his walk-in closets still provide abundant space. He was the first to put telephones in bedrooms, devised indirect lighting systems for the restaurant, and included double glazing and electric clocks. Much of his forethought has been kept today. Although the latest in hotel telephone systems has recently been installed at the Ritz, the old bell pushes, with which to call maid or valet, still lie by the bedside.

Ritz hated lobbies which he said encouraged loiterers and instead created something of an indoor garden in Edwardian rococo splendour. The Palm Court is now a fashionable spot for cocktails, sipping pink champagne or taking afternoon tea at high, round tables topped with Ritz-monogrammed Irish linen, and it epitomises the era's interiors. The Palm Court is stepped up from the gallery that runs through the hotel to the restaurant. It has a wrought-iron and glass roof, and false windows, flanked by potted palms. A hundred-year-old, double, Persian garden carpet covers the floor and the original rose and green colour scheme is highlighted by gilding and a fountain focal point; a gold-leafed figure of La Source with attendant water nymphs.

At the Green Park end of the hotel is the restaurant which shows perfectly the French influence of the time. The room looks out over Green Park and a small sunken Italianate garden, surfaced with astro-turf, which is used for private parties and wedding receptions. A herb garden has been established here for the use of the Ritz kitchens. The dining room, which seats 150, is a copy of a salon in the Palace of Versailles. The murals are inspired by the works of de Neufforge and the ceiling alone took two years to paint with a pale blue sky and fluffy clouds. It is hung with huge swags of brass garlands linking gilded chandeliers and the whole is supported by pink pillars.

Opening off the dining room is the Marie Antoinette Room used for breakfast service and private dinner parties. During the war, its windows were boarded up and it was used for meetings between Churchill, Eisenhower and De Gaulle. It also acted, along with the ladies' room, as an air raid shelter for the exiled princes and princesses and their children who lived at the Ritz at that time.

Cesar Ritz, lured to London initially by Rupert D'Oyly Carte of Gilbert and Sullivan fame, brought with him the great chef, Escoffier, and established a very classical French cuisine at his hotel. Escoffier named his dishes after the famous diners he served; à la carte eating was originated, and it became fashionable for ladies to eat out in hotels.

But in 1981, a breath of British air blew into the hallowed Ritz kitchens. Michael Quinn, in his mid-thirties, became the first British chef to rule the Ritz kitchens. He was commissioned to reorganise and update the kitchens since little had changed since the days of Escoffier. By chance, rather than design, the brigade of 38 'white hats', with the exception of a single Swiss cook, is all British and the total kitchen staff numbers 48. Michael Quinn emphasises the need for team work in the kitchen and personally inspects every dish that goes out of the kitchen. He also helps train many apprentices. With only two small function rooms to serve, the food can be supervised with great care.

Quinn has restored the menu to English and is opposed to the Escoffier custom of naming dishes. He feels this means the dish has to be identical each time it is cooked and this inhibits chefs from expressing their own ideas and prohibits flexibility with ingredients and flavours. He prefers just a brief description of the dish to go on the menu and uses only fresh ingredients.

Like Chef Bainbridge, Michael Quinn started his cookery career as an apprentice at the age of 15 years. He then studied at the Leeds College of Food and Technology on a day-release scheme from the Queen's Hotel, Leeds and was named top Apprentice Chef of Great Britain in 1966. Since then, he has worked at hotels like Claridges, the Garden House in Cambridge, Kildwick Hall, and the Bridge Inn, Walshford (both in Yorkshire), as a lecturer in professional cookery at the Bear Hotel, Woodstock, near Oxford and finally as Chef de Cuisine at Gravetye Manor in Sussex before joining the Ritz.

As well as transforming the Ritz menu with light, attractively presented dishes with exquisite sauces, Michael Quinn has redesigned the basement kitchens, brightening the area, putting in new cookers raised on pedestals that are easy to clean around, new store-rooms, a tiled hot-plate area and work areas with fridges with sliding doors underneath. New Royal Doulton china and cloches for the dishes with the Ritz lion logo on are also being introduced. Proudly, a notice at either entrance to the kitchens states, 'You are now entering the Ritz kitchens' and on request the chef is pleased to show guests around. Food writers often come to take a mid-afternoon lunch with Quinn and his sous chefs in the chef's office lined with Quinn's culinary awards, copper pans, a portrait of Cesar Ritz and shelves filled with beautifully arranged bottled fruits and truffles.

Like the herb garden which is now well enough established to make the Ritz self sufficient in certain herbs, Michael Quinn has also introduced the idea of bottling items. He bought 48 lbs/24 kg of fresh French black truffles last year for about 585 dollars; a year's supply. These were bottled in the kitchens, steamed for 25–30 hours in a equal mixture of veal stock and Madeira and then packed in jars graded in size. Next year he wants to bottle even more and perhaps make jars available to Ritz guests. Varieties of fruit are also bottled.

In late 1982, Michael Quinn travelled on the QE2 and for two evenings demonstrated his recipes in the Queen's Grill and several of these recipes, such as **Breast of Duckling with Fish Vermouth Sauce and Fresh Crab, Duck Fantail with Watercress and Crayfish Sauce** and a starter of poached pear with smoked salmon and lemon mint dressing, are now on the ship's special order list. Chef Quinn also presented this **Jerusalem Artichoke Soup** on the QE2.

Jerusalem Artichoke Soup   *serves 4*

3 oz/75 g butter
1 lb/450 g Jerusalem artichokes, washed and peeled   *(continued)*

Melt butter in a large pan and add all the chopped vegetables. Cook gently for 4–5 minutes so the vegetables soften but are not browned. Add the flour

¼ cup/2 oz/50 g chopped celery
⅙ cup/1 oz/25 g chopped shallots
⅙ cup/1 oz/25 g chopped leeks
½ cup/2 oz/50 g flour
4¼ cups plus 2 tbs/1¾ pints/1 litre
    chicken stock
salt, freshly ground black pepper
½ cup plus 2 tbs/¼ pint/150 ml heavy
    (double) cream
1 egg
small quantity white wine
pinch fresh, chopped chives
pinch fresh, chopped tarragon
chopped chives to garnish
cream to finish

and stir in well, cooking for a further 2 minutes. Add the stock, blend in well and season to taste. Simmer for 20 minutes. Remove from the heat and put contents of the pan through a sieve or blender until smooth and puréed. Add cream, beaten egg and wine and check the seasoning. Allow soup to become cold and serve with spoonfuls of cream on top of each serving sprinkled with chopped chives.

At the Ritz, the monthly bill for fresh vegetables alone is around 1,900 dollars (and an equivalent amount is spent on meat). Two contrasting ways of making use of seasonal vegetables are in a **Vegetable and Hot Crispy Bacon Salad** and a **Terrine of Leeks.**

Vegetable and Hot Crispy Bacon Salad

serves 4

4 oz/125 g French beans
4 oz/125 g sugar peas
2 artichoke bottoms, sliced thinly
8–10 raw, young spinach leaves
1 avocado pear, peeled and sliced thinly
salt, freshly ground black pepper
4 rashers back bacon
for the sherry or wine vinegar dressing:
1 part sherry or white wine vinegar
2 parts walnut oil
1 tsp/5 ml English mustard
¼ oz/7 g finely chopped fresh herbs
salt, pepper to taste

Lightly cook all the vegetables in a little butter and season to taste with salt and pepper. Mix together in a large bowl. For the dressing, whisk all the dressing ingredients together and add to the vegetables in the bowl. (Chef Quinn recommends the use of walnut oil if possible; if not, use olive oil). The salad can be chilled in the fridge for up to an hour before serving. Finally grill the bacon until it is crisp. Chop into bite-sized pieces and serve scattered on top of the salad.

Terrine of Leeks

serves 4

12 young leeks of the same size
butter to cook
salt, pepper   *(continued)*

Trim tops and tails of the leeks and remove the two outside leaves. Slice lengthways and wash under warm running water, making sure all the earth and grit is removed. Butter an ovenproof dish small enough to pack the leeks in tightly. Place the leeks in

for the sauce:
1 part sherry or white wine vinegar
2 parts olive oil
1 tsp/5 ml English mustard
¼ oz/7 g finely chopped shallots
freshly chopped herbs
salt, freshly ground black pepper to taste

the dish, pressing them down firmly, season with salt and pepper and coat generously with melted butter. Cover the dish with foil. Bring to the boil and cook gently on top of the stove for 3–4 minutes. Lift the foil and loosen the leeks with a sharp knife. Place the dish in a bain marie (in a roasting dish half full of water) in the oven and cook at 325F/170C/Gas 3 for 25 minutes. Remove from the oven and allow dish with leeks to cool. Place a weight on the foil to press down the leeks while they are cooling in the fridge. When really chilled, slice the leeks crossways. Place on a plate and coat gently with the sauce made by whisking all the sauce ingredients together.

The Ritz menus often feature a sorbet not only as a dessert with a coulis of fruit, but also as a throat-refresher, Edwardian style between courses. This one would be suitable, though in fact, at the Ritz, it is served as an appetiser.

Gazpacho Sorbet　　　　　　　　　*serves 6*

6 portions Gazpacho soup (see page 22) but omitting garlic and using less olive oil than usual
1 egg white
sprigs of mint
finely chopped red and green peppers for garnish

Make **Gazpacho Soup** to the recipe on page 22 but leave out garlic and add only a little oil. Place in a plastic container and freeze until mixture is mushy. Stiffly beat the egg white and fold into the mixture. (The proportion of egg whites is roughly 1 for every 5–6 portions). Pile mixture back into container and re-freeze. Serve in glasses decorated with a sprig of mint and garnished with finely chopped red and green peppers.

Fresh Pear Vinaigrette　　　　　　*serves 6*

6 ripe pears
½ cup plus 2 tbs/¼ pint/150 ml white wine vinegar　　　　　　*(continued)*

Peel the pears using a vegetable peeler, leaving the stalk attached. Place in a saucepan, add the vinegar,

10 fresh mint leaves plus 6 for garnish
10 fresh tarragon leaves
for smoked ham dressing:
2½ fl oz/62 ml white wine vinegar
½ oz/13 g fresh mint and tarragon
juice of 2 lemons
salt, pepper, caster sugar to taste
3 oz/75 g smoked ham

mint and tarragon. Add just enough water to cover and poach gently until the pears are tender. Drain off the liquid and leave pears to become cold. Make the dressing by mixing vinegar, finely chopped mint and tarragon, and lemon juice with salt, pepper and caster sugar to taste. Cut the ham into strips and blend in. Slice the top off each pear and put on one side. Carefully scoop out the core and fill the centre with the smoked ham dressing. Replace the top of the pear. Remove the stalk and replace with a fresh mint leaf. Serve with the remainder of the dressing or with a mayonnaise lightly creamed with chopped mint and tarragon leaves and flavoured with a little fresh lemon juice.

Like the QE2, the Ritz is a place to find good caviare. Michael Quinn has devised this **Caviare and Dill Dressing** which he serves with avocado pear and smoked salmon mousse; the mousse is piped around the half avocado. The dressing would go well with many green salads.

Caviare and Dill Dressing

makes about ½ cup/4 fl oz/125 ml

¼ cup/1 oz/25 g very finely chopped
  onion
1–1½ tbs/15–22 ml white wine vinegar
2 tsps/10 ml olive oil
2 tsps/10 ml hazelnut oil
1 tsp/5 ml fresh chopped chives, parsley,
  dill, or tarragon
salt (a pinch, or to taste), freshly ground
  black pepper
2 tsps/10 ml caviare

Whisk the onion, vinegar oil and chopped herbs together until well blended. Stir in the salt and pepper to taste. Carefully stir in the caviare. Serve tossed with salad greens or spooned over avocado slices.

Each day, both for lunch and dinner, Michael Quinn has introduced a Surprise Menu of four inclusive courses and which is changed every two weeks. The dishes are based on what is currently best from the markets and, if the diner insists, details will be given by the Head Waiter, but most just sit back and wait to be pleasantly surprised. The following two recipes come from Quinn's Surprise Menu lists.

Boned Best End of Lamb with Artichoke Bottoms

serves 4

3 best ends of lamb
4 Globe artichokes
1 tb/15 ml lemon juice or wine vinegar
for the lamb stock sauce:
lamb bones and pieces from above
fresh root vegetables in season
fresh herbs such as tarragon, pinch of
*   thyme*
butter (unsalted)
salt, pepper

Remove the 'eye' of the meat from each lamb cutlet and put on one side. Place bones and the rest of the lamb pieces in a hot oven until they become golden brown. Put them in a pan with roughly chopped root vegetables, herbs and seasoning and cover with cold water. Simmer until the stock acquires a dark colour and a rich flavour. Strain stock and continue cooking until it is reduced to the consistency of a coating sauce. Before serving as a sauce, beat in a generous amount of unsalted butter to thicken. Adjust seasoning to taste. Meanwhile, wash artichokes and remove tough outer leaves. Place in boiling salted water to which 1 tb/15 ml lemon juice has been added (or wine vinegar). Cook for 20 minutes. Allow to cool and remove leaves and choke. Trim the 'eyes' of lamb of all sinew and fat. Season with salt and freshly ground black pepper. Place in an ovenproof dish which has been brushed with oil in a hot oven (450F/240C/Gas 8). Place the meat in the heated dish and cook in the oven for 5 minutes when the meat will be pink. If it is preferred to have the meat well done, allow a further 4 minutes in the oven. Allow the meat to rest for 3–4 minutes in warm place before serving. To serve, coat the warmed serving plates with the sauce. Slice the warmed artichoke bottoms very thin horizontally and arrange in a fan shape on the plate. Slice the meat thinly and fan out on top of the artichoke slices. Decorate with a few fresh tarragon leaves or fresh chives or chopped scallion (spring onion) tops.

Breast of Pheasant with Chestnuts and Ginger Wine
serves 4

2 hen pheasants
for the sauce:
pheasant carcase and trimmings from
*   above*
fresh root vegetables, roughly chopped
fresh herbs, such as sprig of thyme, ½
*   bay leaf, parsley stalks*
ginger wine
unsalted butter
salt, pepper to taste
1 lb/450 g fresh chestnuts
chicken stock
2–3 celery stalks
oil
butter
watercress for garnish

Remove the breasts from the pheasants and divide into 4 portions. Roast the remaining pheasant carcases and trimmings in a hot oven in a roasting pan until brown. Remove from the oven and place in a pan with roughly chopped, root vegetables, herbs and seasoning, and cover with cold water. Bring to the boil and simmer until the stock becomes dark in colour and has a rich flavour. Strain and add a generous measure of ginger wine. Reduce stock to half its amount and before serving as a sauce, remove to the side of the stove and whisk in some unsalted butter to thicken. Check seasoning to taste. Meanwhile, slit the chestnuts and place in a tin in a hot oven for a few minutes to loosen the skin. Shell the chestnuts and put them in a pan of chicken stock with chopped celery. Bring to the boil and cook for 3–4 minutes. Leave in the stock until cooked (the chestnuts will still be firm). Season the pheasant breasts with sea salt and freshly ground black pepper. Brush a flameproof dish with oil and heat in the oven at 450F/230C/Gas 8. Add a small piece of butter and put the pheasant in it and seal quickly on top of the stove. Place in the hot oven and cook for 10–15 minutes turning the pieces of pheasant after 10 minutes. Remove from the oven, take out the meat and leave to rest in a warm place. Drain the fat from the dish and put in the chestnuts. The dish will be hot and dry and contain the sediment left by the pheasant. Add some butter and cook the chestnuts for about 2–3 minutes on top of the stove turning them, and drain very well. Place a mound of chestnuts in the centre of a heated serving dish, and surround with the sliced breasts of pheasant. Put the sauce on one side of the dish and keep some to serve separately. Decorate meat with watercress.

Opposite: Above: The Ritz Hotel Restaurant.

Below: Michael Quinn, Head Chef at the Ritz, puts the finishing touches to the avocado pear and smoked salmon mousse.

Partridge with Caramelised Apples, Cream and Calvados Sauce

serves 4

4 partridge
celery, parsley, salt, tarragon for
    partridge insides
fat to bard
for the sauce:
generous measure Calvados
1¼ cups/½ pint/275 ml heavy (double)
    cream
salt, freshly ground black pepper
3 oz/75 g unsalted butter
caramelised apples:
4 apples peeled, quartered, and shaped
    like small barrels and blanched in
    boiling water for a minute or two and
    then well dried
juice of 1 lemon
¼ cup/2 oz/50 g sugar
a little cold water

Sprinkle herbs, salt and chopped celery inside the partridge and seal the partridge in a large skillet (frying pan) on top of the stove. Place in a roasting dish in a preheated oven at 450F/230C/Gas 8 and cook on both sides allowing 5 minutes for each side and finish with 5 minutes with the bird on its back. Remove the strips of fat used for barding (covering the breast, etc) after 2 minutes. Keep the flesh pink. Remove from the pan and allow to rest in a warm place while making the sauce. Make the sauce by straining fat from the pan and keeping the partridge sediment. Swill out the pan with Calvados (be very generous with this says Chef Quinn), reduce the amount of liquid by half, add the cream and reduce again until of coating consistency. Season to taste with salt and pepper and finally thicken with the unsalted butter. Prepare the apples by blanching and keeping white by brushing with the lemon juice. Boil together the sugar and water and reduce the amount until almost like caramel. Throw in the apples and cook for 1 minute. Remove from the sauce and keep warm. To serve, drain off excess fat carefully and place partridge on a serving dish. Coat with the Calvados sauce poured through a fine strainer, decorate with the apples and garnish with fresh watercress and fresh truffle slices if available.

In London on August 12th many hotels compete to be the first to serve grouse on the day that the official shooting season opens. But the Ritz feels that for the best flavour the grouse should be hung for several days before eating. Young grouse are usually roasted but Michael Quinn describes how to marinate and pan-cook this bird and serve with a wild mushrooms and cream sauce along with a side-salad of cucumber.

Grouse with Wild Mushroom Sauce and Cucumber Salad

serves 4

2 young grouse, plucked, drawn, washed inside and dried
for marinade:
2 glasses red wine with crushed black peppercorns, bay leaf, sprig of thyme
2 oz/50 g chopped carrots, celery and fennel
1 tb/15 ml olive oil
salt, freshly ground black pepper
oil and butter to cook
for the sauce:
½ oz/13 g butter
½ oz/13 g finely chopped shallots
4 oz/125 g wild mushrooms (Chanterelle, Cepes)
2 measures port wine
½ cup plus 2 tbs/¼ pint/150 ml heavy (double) cream
sea salt, freshly ground black pepper
1 tsp/5 ml grated horseradish
1 tsp/5 ml chopped fresh tarragon, chives, parsley
for cucumber salad:
1 cucumber
salt
white wine vinegar
freshly ground black pepper

Marinate the grouse in the mixture of red wine, peppercorns, bay leaf, herbs, chopped carrots, celery and fennel and olive oil for 48 hours. Remove grouse from mixture and dry thoroughly. Remove the legs and carefully remove the breast from the carcase. Season with salt and pepper. Reheat a pan until hot and add a little oil and butter to coat the bottom of the pan. When sizzling, add the grouse thighs and cook for 3 minutes, turning occasionally. Keep the flesh moist. Add the breasts to the pan and cook for a further 3 minutes. Coat with the sauce and sprnkle with the fresh chopped herbs. To make the sauce, preheat a small pan until hot and put in the butter. Add shallots and cook for 1 minute, stirring with a wooden spoon. Add the washed, cleaned mushrooms and cook for 2 minutes. Add port wine and cook until the amount is reduced by half. Add cream, salt, and pepper and continue to reduce until the mixture is of coating consistency. Finally, add the horseradish and check the seasoning. Keep warm until ready to coat the meat.

Serve with buttered fresh noodles and a well chilled cucumber salad.

To make cucumber salad: peel the cucumber and slice extremely thin. Place the cucumber in a bowl and sprinkle with a little salt and leave in the fridge for 4 hours. Drain thoroughly and add a little ground pepper and some white wine vinegar to taste. Serve very chilled.

Duck is another bird which makes a frequent appearance on the Ritz dining table.

Fantail of Duck with a Leek and Spinach Sauce

serves 2

2 duck breasts
4 white parts of leeks
1 oz/25 g butter
1¼ cups/½ pint/275 ml chicken stock
2 oz/50 g leaf spinach
salt, pepper
8 pieces mange tout
½ cup plus 2 tbs/¼ pint/150 ml heavy
    (double) cream
salt, pepper
small bunch chopped chives
truffle (optional)

Remove duck breasts from the carcase and trim off any sinew but leave skin on. Remove fillets from inside the main breasts. Clean and wash the white parts of the leeks and the spinach. Cut up leek roughly and place in a pan with butter and cook until softened but not browned. Add chicken stock and simmer. When nearly cooked, add the spinach and simmer for a few minutes, season to taste; then liquidize and pass purée through a sieve. Cut five mange tout in half diagonally across and then cut the remaining mange tout into very thin strips, about 1½ in/3½ cm long and put on one side. Heat a pan, add seasoned duck pieces and cook on both sides keeping the meat pink and lastly, adding the two fillets. Heat the vegetable purée, add the cream, season to taste and keep on the side of the stove. Slice the breast of duck lengthways into five or six slices. Dip the mange tout into boiling water and pat dry. Place the cream sauce on the bottom of the plate, sprinkle chopped chives around the edge and arrange the slices of duck and mange tout in a fan shape. Add the rest of the small strips of mange tout and truffle slices if used, and serve.

Sole with Langoustines, Avocado and Tomato

serves 4

4 Dover sole of about 12–16 oz/350–
    450 g each, skinned and the heads
    removed
salt, freshly ground black pepper
flour to coat
clarified butter
8 oz shelled fresh langoustines (Dublin
    Bay prawns or scampi): if not
    available fresh use fresh 'ordinary',
    European prawns, not frozen
    langoustines   *(continued)*

Season the fish and dip them in flour. Shake off excess flour and brush both sides of the fish with clarified butter. Grill for about 5 minutes on each side. Brush occasionally with the butter. When cooked, keep hot on a large plate. Toss together, the tomatoes, langoustines and avocado, in clarified butter. Season to taste and add citrus juice. Arrange garnish on the soles and sprinkle with chives before serving.

½ cup/4 oz/125 g skinned, deseeded and chopped tomatoes
4 oz/125 g skinned and sliced avocado pear
1 tsp/5 ml freshly chopped chives (or tarragon)
juice of ½ lemon or lime

The herbs such as basil, bay, thyme, tarragon, chives, parsley and chervil grown in the Ritz's small parkside garden are used in many dishes and sauces. In one idea, freshly chopped basil, chives, tarragon, parsley and rosemary are used sprinkled on trimmed and seasoned veal cutlets which are cooked briskly and lightly in a little butter, removed from the heat, excess fat drained off and the pan swilled with dry vermouth and lemon juice and more herbs. Finally ½ cup/4 oz/125 g butter is whisked in to create a simple, but tasty sauce for the veal.

Michael Croft, who lives in Bromley in Kent, works mainly on sauces which have some nouvelle cuisine influence in being reductions not roux and sauces at the Ritz are served around, not over, the meat. Michael Croft trained at the prestigious Westminster College in London and worked at the Connaught Hotel and Gravetye Manor, the latter with Michael Quinn, before coming to the Ritz. He has also worked as an Egon Ronay inspector and so knows how to judge a dish severely.

Breast of Chicken with Fresh Crabmeat

serves 4

A sauce with an unusual fish and fowl flavour blend for breast of chicken.

4 chicken breasts, skin, fat and sinew removed
butter to cook   *(continued)*

Preheat a flameproof pan and add a piece of butter. Cook the chicken breasts, with the outside downwards, quickly for 3–4 minutes then turn and

sherry glass of vermouth
1¼ cups/½ pint/275 ml heavy (double)
  cream
salt, freshly ground black pepper
4 tbs/60 ml fresh crabmeat
1 oz/25 g butter
watercress to garnish

cook the other side for the same time. Remove chicken from pan and keep in a warm place. Strain off excess fat from the pan and pour in the vermouth. Let it boil for 2–3 minutes to reduce the amount. Add salt and pepper to taste and cream and bring to the boil again and reduce the amount slightly. Add the crabmeat and allow to heat thoroughly. Bring pan to side of stove and whisk in butter to thicken the sauce and give it a glossy finish. Check seasoning. Serve chicken coated with the sauce and garnished with watercress.

Michael Quinn, a twin and the youngest of eight children, started cooking at home as a child and his four sisters were happy to let him help with the cookery chores. He still loves the traditional British puddings he learnt from this mother and includes many on the Ritz menus, like steamed **Roly-poly Pudding, Queen of Puddings** and **Apple Charlotte.**

Quinn's mother used to make puddings for her hungry brood based often on left overs in the fridge and one of her favourites was the humble, yet tasty **Bread and Butter Pudding.** Michael helped his mother make this recipe to which, at the Ritz, he has added a few touches of luxury.

Ritz Bread and Butter Pudding   *serves 4*

8 slices white bread
unsalted butter to butter bread
¼ cup/2 oz/50 g sultanas
5 eggs
1 cup/8 oz/225 g caster sugar
1¼ cups/½ pint/275 ml milk
1¼ cups/½ pint/275 ml heavy (double)
  cream
vanilla pod
nutmeg

Remove crusts from bread slices and butter them. Cut bread in triangles. Place bread in a buttered ovenproof dish and put sultanas between each layer of bread. Beat eggs and sugar together until well mixed. Bring milk and cream to the boil with the vanilla pod. Strain the milk and cream onto the beaten eggs and sugar very gently, and mix thoroughly. Strain through a fine strainer into a pouring jug. Pour half of the liquid on the bread in the ovenproof dish being careful not to disturb the shape of the bread. Leave for 7–8 minutes to allow the bread to absorb all the flavour. Top with the rest of the liquid. Sprinkle with nutmeg. Stand the dish in a roasting tin of hot water coming halfway up the dish sides and bake in the oven at 325F/170C/Gas 3 for 35–40 minutes. When the pudding is set and ready it should be firm to the touch. If it is not, cook for a little longer.

Mark Steeden, who lives at Broadstairs in Kent, attended the Thanet Training College and worked at Grosvenor House and the Dorchester before coming to the Ritz in 1982. He also spent a season in Australia working at one of Kerry Packer's ski resorts in the Blue Mountains. Mark Steeden tends to devote himself to creating delicious desserts such as a cold Drambuie cream in a thin biscuit case surrounded by a raspberry coulis. This **Pink Champagne Sabayon with Exotic Fruits** and the **Crème de Menthe Iced Soufflé** are examples of his work.

Pink Champagne Sabayon with Exotic Fruits

serves 4–6

6 egg yolks
1 whole egg
¾ cup plus 1 tb/5 oz/150 g icing sugar
1¼ cups/½ pint/275 ml pink champagne
exotic fruits as available: sliced mango, fresh fig, strawberries, lychee, nectarine
icing sugar to dust

Whisk the egg yolks, whole egg and sugar together in a bowl over hot water until light and frothy. Whisk in the pink champagne. Peel and slice fruits as available and arrange decoratively on a plate. Sprinkle a few passion fruit seeds (if available) over the fruit and cover the fruit with sabayon egg mixture. Dust with icing sugar and place under a hot grill for a few moments to brown. The fruit should stay cold but the sabayon remain warm.

Crème de Menthe Iced Soufflé

serves 4

3 egg yolks
½ cup/4 oz/125 g sugar
1¼ cups/½ pint/275 ml heavy (double) cream
½ cup/4 fl oz/125 ml crème de menthe
3 egg whites
icing sugar to dust

Whisk the egg yolks until light and frothy. Cook the sugar with a little water until syrupy (the soft ball stage). Whisk the sugar onto the yolks and add the crème de menthe and whisk until cold. Fold in the cream which has been whipped to a soft, thick consistency. Whisk egg white until stiff and firm. Fold into the mixture. Place mixture in individual soufflé dishes fitted with a paper collar. Freeze until set. To serve, remove paper collar, scoop out a small hollow on top of the soufflé and fill with crème de menthe. Dust the top with icing sugar and serve with almond biscuits.

Apple Charlotte

serves 4–6

Named after one of England's Hanoverian queens.

thinly sliced white bread
½ cup/4 oz/125 g butter
2 lb/1 kg cooking apples
7 oz/200 g brown sugar
½ cup/4 oz/125 g sultanas
½ oz/13 g ground cinnamon
apricot jam to glaze

Cut the bread into fingers and dip one side in some of the butter which has been melted. Arrange bread in a small, round, shallow ovenproof dish, placing buttered side against the dish sides. Peel, core and slice apples and place in a saucepan. Add the sugar, cinnamon, sultanas and remainder of the butter. Cook briskly until the apples are half cooked. Place in the bread lined dish and cover with more buttered bread. Bake in a hot oven 425F/220C/Gas 7 until bread is golden brown. Turn out onto a warm serving dish and glaze with melted apricot jam. Serve hot with a vanilla sauce.

Vienna Cream

serves 6–8

1 lb/450 g cream cheese
½ cup/4 oz/125 g caster sugar
2 tbs/30 ml milk   *(continued)*

Blend the cream cheese, sugar and milk together until creamy and soft. Add at least half of the sherry or other liqueur a little at a time, then more to taste.

*4–6 tbs/60–90 ml sweet sherry to taste
(or rum or cherry brandy)*
*toasted almond slivers (optional) to
garnish*

(The liquor taste will get stronger with time). Fill 6–8 wine glasses with the mixture and chill in the fridge for at least 2 hours. (The mixture will keep for 2 days). The dish can be served as a dessert topping instead of cream, or as a filling for chocolate sponge cake or profiteroles; for this add 1–1½/15–22 ml lemon juice as the flavouring instead of the liqueur.

Acknowledgements

The author would like to thank the ship's company of the *Queen Elizabeth 2* for their co-operation and help in providing information for this book. In particular on the QE2 thanks to Chef John Bainbridge and his staff for the hours of time devoted daily to discussion of recipes on a busy World Cruise section. To Hotel Manager, John Duffy and his staff, and the Cruise Director Bob Haines and his staff. At the Ritz hotel, London, thanks to Chef de Cuisine, Michael Quinn, his sous chefs and to Thama Davies.

The author would also like to thank the directors of Cunard on both sides of the Atlantic for their assistance in providing facilities to gather information and to Alice Marshall and Susan Alpert in Cunard's New York office for their help with photographic research. Finally, to Dianne Coles of Gulliver Publishing who worked so hard to get the book into being and who was such a lively travelling companion on the QE2.

Measures and Materials

Working out the measurements just proves how, even in cooking, we beg to differ from nation to nation. Oscar Wilde once said that the US and the UK were one nation divided by a common language and in kitchen terms this seems very true.

In the book, I have put American measures first, followed by Imperial (British) measures where these are different. Finally there is a metric conversion. In making up any of these recipes, the cook should stick to only one set of measurements.

On the QE2, the chefs work in Imperial measures ussing as a base the 10 fl oz British cup measure (2 cups equal 1 Imperial pint of 20 fl oz). The American cup equals 8 fl oz (2 cups equals one American pint of 16 fl oz). The British tablespoon measure is also slightly larger than an American tablespoon (and the Australian is slightly smaller). But differences between the American and British tablespoons are so small (2 UK equals 3 US) that I have used equivalent measures throughout. For the metric conversion I have used a base of 25 g to 1 oz and 450 g to 1 lb; and for liquid measure a base of 150 ml to ¼ pint (UK) ½ cup plus 2 tabs for US — 757 ml to 1 UK pint; 2½ cups US.

Kitchen vocabulary also varies and where common differences occur I have put the American term first in the ingredients lists followed by the British term in brackets; eg ground (minced), heavy (double) cream or cornstarch (cornflour), and continued using the American term only, in the recipe method. Flour used in the recipes is all-purpose (plain).

For thickening, arrowroot or cornstarch can be used as preferred and for recipes using gelatine the ship uses sheet gelatine now available in most places. The QE2 does not sweeten any of the whipped cream used in her sweet recipes and in the book no sugar has been added to the cream mentioned. The ship uses unsalted (sweet) butter for its recipes and adjustments in seasoning should be made according to personal taste.

Some other culinary dictionary definitions of ingredients used in the book can be noted for they are not always translated in the text:

American	British	American	British
waxed paper	greaseproof paper	blend	liquidise
mold	mould	package	packet
pastry bag	piping bag	eggplant	aubergine
bacon slice	bacon rasher	cookie/cracker	biscuit
purple grapes	black grapes	white grapes	green grapes
ripe olives	black olives	celery stalk	celery stick
chili pepper	chili	baking apple	cooking apple
brown sugar	demerara	extract	essence
gelatin	gelatine	cured or smoked bacon	ham
hard-cooked eggs	hard-boiled eggs	shortening	lard
ground	minced	heavy cream	double cream
light cream	single cream	cornstarch	cornflour
shelled shrimp	peeled prawn	shrimps	prawns
ginger root	root ginger	seeded raisins	seedless raisins
white raisins	sultanas	summer squash	pumpkin
light brown sugar	soft brown sugar	scallion	spring onion
bouillon cube	stock cube	bouillon/broth	stock
corn	sweetcorn	tomato paste	tomato purée
vanilla bean	vanilla pod	skillet	frying pan
broil	grill	pan-fry	shallow-fry
confectioners' sugar	icing sugar	baking soda	bicarbonate of soda
baker's chocolate (US is darker and one square equals an ounce)	cooking chocolate	beef tenderloin	fillet
		boston or navy beans	haricot beans
contrefillet	sirloin	frosting	icing
cornmeal	polenta	Romaine lettuce	cos lettuce
jelly	jam		
string beans	French or runner beans		

Index